LOLITA

A Janus Text

TWAYNE'S MASTERWORK STUDIES

Robert Lecker, Editor

LOLITA

A Janus Text

Lance Olsen

TWAYNE PUBLISHERS
An Imprint of Simon & Schuster Macmillan
New York

Prentice Hall International
London Mexico City New Delhi Singapore Sydney Toronto

Twayne's Masterwork Studies No. 153

Lolita: A Janus Text
Lance Olsen

Twayne Publishers
An Imprint of Simon & Schuster Macmillan
866 Third Avenue
New York, NY 10022

Library of Congress Cataloging-in-Publication Data

Olsen, Lance, 1956–
    Lolita : a Janus text / Lance Olsen.
       p.   cm.—(Twayne's masterworks studies; MWS 153)
    Includes bibliographical references and index.
    ISBN 0-8057-8355-5—ISBN 0-8057-8593-0 (pbk.)
    1. Nabokov, Vladimir Vladimirovich, 1899–1977. I. Title. II. Series.
PS3527.A15L6347 1995
813'.54—dc20   94-24562
                                                                           CIP

The paper used in this publication meets the minimum requirements of American
National Standard for Information Sciences—Permanence of Paper for Printed Library
Materials, ANSI Z39.48-1984.

10 9 8 7 6 5 4 3 2 1 (hc)
10 9 8 7 6 5 4 3 2   (pbk)

Printed in the United States of America.

For—who else?
—Andrea

Contents

Vladimir Nabokov.
Illustration by Andi Olsen.

Note on the References
and Acknowledgments

Why would anyone want to amass extra pages on *Lolita* more than half a century after its initial publication by a pretty seedy French porn house? David Rampton, in his book on Nabokov, reminds us that Frederick Crews in *The Pooh Perplex* holds that our goal in literary criticism is to collect as much commentary around a work as possible, just to show we care. I confess this was my motivation for composing what comes next: it is a means of paying my respects to, and entering the vibrant conversation about, a novel I have adored since I originally discovered it as an undergraduate at the University of Wisconsin in my first course (taught by John Lyons) concerning contemporary American fiction.

Before beginning, a few pedestrian points. First, all references to Nabokov's text are taken from the revised and updated *Annotated Lolita* (New York: Vintage Books, 1991), first published in 1970, a marvelous if pricey scholarly edition of the novel meticulously edited, elegantly introduced, and helpfully annotated by Alfred Appel, Jr., Nabokov's friend and former student at Cornell. For a less dear edition perhaps more appropriate for classroom use, there is the Vintage International incarnation (New York: Vintage, 1989). Page references to the *Annotated Lolita* are noted parenthetically in the text, as are those to *Strong Opinions* (New York: Vintage Books, 1990). All other sources are cited in the notes.

Second, some of the central ideas in this study concerning the double nature of *Lolita* first stirred in my essay entitled "A Janus-Text: Realism, Fantasy, and Nabokov's *Lolita*," which initially appeared in

Modern Fiction Studies 32, no. 1 (Spring 1986): 115–26, and then reappeared substantially metamorphosed in my chapter on *Lolita* in *Circus of the Mind in Motion: Postmodernism and the Comic Vision* (Detroit: Wayne State University Press, 1990).

Last, I wish to extend my warm thanks to Gary Williams, fine friend and champion chair of the English department at the University of Idaho, for his resonant support in numerous ways while I wrote this book, including generously granting me course reductions in the fall of 1993 and spring of 1994; and, as always, to Andrea, instrumental now for nearly a decade and a half in helping me daily compose my own love story.

Chronology: Vladimir Nabokov's Life and Works

1899   Vladimir Vladimirovich Nabokov, first of five children, born into an aristocratic family with 50 servants in St. Petersburg, Russia, 10 April in the Old Style or Julian calendar, 22 April in the New Style or Gregorian. (With the century's turn, the Old Style falls another day behind the New, placing Nabokov's birthday on 23 April—the same as Shakespeare's and Shirley Temple's.) His father, Vladimir Dmitrievich Nabokov, is a liberal, widely traveled, and well-educated (his library contains 10,000 books) scholar of criminal law, politician, and political journalist, whom Nabokov adores. His mother, Elena Ivanovna Rukavishnikov, is a lover of modern poetry whose wealthy family made its fortune in mining.

1906   Nabokov discovers butterflies while summering at family estate at Vyra, commencing lifelong passion for lepidoptery.

1911   Enters Tenishev School, one of best and most emphatically progressive private Russian academies. A rowdy, adventurous trilingual Anglophile, Nabokov grows up in a bright universe of French and English governesses and personal valets, wintering in St. Petersburg, summering at Vyra, autumning on the coasts of southern Europe. Plays soccer and tennis. Boxes, fences, skis, bikes. Adores chess (another lifelong passion). Draws so well his parents assume he will become a painter. Writes poetry in Russian, French, and English.

1914–1918 During World War I, falls in love with neighbor, Valentina Eugenievna Shulgin ("Tamara" in autobiography, "Mary" in first novel); in 1916 self-publishes first book of poems: 68 poems dedicated to Valentina. Inherits equivalent of several million dollars and 2,000-acre estate from his uncle, Vasily Rukavishnikov. In 1917, after Bolsheviks storm Winter Palace and seize power, flees with his family to estate in Crimea, still a free area. In 1918, with friend, publishes second book of poems.

1919   In April, sees last of Russia when family, now suddenly poor, flees Crimea for London. In October, supported by scholarships, enters Trinity College, Cambridge, where he studies French and Russian literature and writes his first English publication ("A Few Notes on Crimean Lepidoptera"), never letting classes interfere with his poems, tennis, and soccer.

1920   Family moves to Berlin. Father helps launch Russian émigré newspaper, *Rul'* (*The Rudder*), responsible for publishing many of Nabokov's poems, plays, stories, reviews, translations, and crossword puzzles.

1922   On 28 March, Nabokov's father shot dead by rightist Russians attempting to assassinate another man. Nabokov graduates from Cambridge with honors. Settles in Berlin, tutoring in French, English, tennis, and boxing. Translates *Alice in Wonderland* into Russian for the equivalent of $5. Joins various writing groups.

1923   Publishes two more books of poems. At charity ball, meets future wife, Véra Evseena Slonim.

1925   Marries Véra, the funny, cultivated, passionately literary daughter of a Jewish lawyer, who becomes his muse, secretary, typist, editor, proofreader, translator, bibliographer, agent, chauffeur, research assistant, and close friend. Long period of living in dingy rented rooms.

1926   Publishes first novel, *Mashen'ka* (*Mary*), under the pen name V. Sirin. Generally unnoticed.

1928   Publishes *Korol', Dama, Valet* (*King, Queen, Knave*). Small but growing critical interest.

1929   Issues *Zashchita Luzhina* (*The Defense*) serially in the prestigious émigré journal *Sovremennye Zapiski* (*Contemporary Annals*) and then as book in 1930.

1930   Publishes stories and poems, *Vozvrashchenie Chorba* (*The Return of Chorb*), and a novella, *Soglyadatay* (*The Eye*).

1931   Issues *Podvig* (*Glory*) serially in *SZ* over next year and as book in 1932. Publishes note on lepidoptery; a handful of others follow during 1940s and 1950s.

1932   Issues *Camera Obscura* (*Laughter in the Dark*) serially in *SZ* over next year and as book in 1933.

Chronology

1949   Learns how to drive.

1950   Begins teaching a course on European fiction that will make his name at Cornell.

1951   Publishes *Conclusive Evidence,* a memoir; revised and expanded version published as *Speak, Memory* in 1966. In summer, begins composing *Lolita* in earnest, often in the backseat of his Oldsmobile parked at a motel on his and Véra's way to Telluride, Colorado, to catch butterflies; collects impressions of America during cross-country trek.

1952   Becomes visiting lecturer in Slavic languages at Harvard.

1953   Receives second Guggenheim Fellowship. Issues *Pnin* serially in the *New Yorker* (1953–55) and as book in 1957. On 6 December, finishes 450-page typescript of *Lolita,* on whose title page no author's name appears.

1955   Following rejection by four American publishers, *Lolita* is brought out in Paris by Olympia Press, known for its pornography, in two-volume edition in Traveller's Companion series. Nabokov receives no reviews or advertisements until Graham Greene chooses *Lolita* in Christmas issue of London *Sunday Times* as one of three best books of year.

1958   *Lolita* published in New York by Putnam's. Nabokov becomes internationally renowned writer at 60. Publishes story collection, *Nabokov's Dozen.*

1959   Stops teaching at Cornell. Sails to Le Havre, never to live in America again. "I never imagined that I should be able to live by my writing, but now I am kept by a little girl named Lolita."

1960   Elected to American National Institute of Arts and Letters. Turns down honor because he never belongs to unions or clubs.

1961   Settles in the elegant Montreux Palace Hotel in Switzerland to be near various family members, including Dmitri, now pursuing opera career in Italy. Retains American citizenship.

1962   Publishes novel *Pale Fire.* Stanley Kubrick's film *Lolita* premieres.

1963   Nabokov nominated for Academy Award for *Lolita* screenplay.

1964   Publishes massive translation and study of *Eugene Onegin.* Its rhymeless literalism sparks an angry reply from Edmund Wilson, beginning one of the fiercest literary feuds of the 1960s while effectively ending the Nabokov-Wilson friendship.

Chronology

LITERARY AND
HISTORICAL CONTEXT

1

Mystery and Minutiae

Vladimir Nabokov (pronounced Vluh-DEEM-ear Nuh-BOK-off) was directly touched by many of the historical spasms that shaped and defined the first half of the twentieth century. He was born into an aristocratic family in St. Petersburg in 1899, six years short of the first Russian revolution, and into a cultural explosion that rivaled those flaring in fin de siècle France, Germany, and England. Modern poetry was thriving, for instance, and by the time Nabokov was 15, he had read most of its practitioners, including the futurists, with their excessively fragmented experimentation (upon which he frowned), and the symbolists, with their vigorous emphasis on individualism, art for art's sake, and the neoromantic impulse to transcend the material world—a constellation of concerns that would be seen nearly 50 years later in Nabokov's twelfth published novel, *Lolita*.

As the Bolsheviks stormed the Winter Palace in October 1917, Nabokov, recently having inherited a 2,000-acre estate and the equivalent of several million dollars, sat at home composing poetry and listening to the gunfire popping a few blocks away. A month later, abruptly cast into near poverty, he and his family were forced to flee to the Crimea and, in 1919, from there to England, where by means of various scholarships Nabokov studied French and Russian literature at Cambridge. After graduation in 1922, he settled in Berlin, another cultural mecca for artists, writers, and scholars such as Maxim Gorky, Boris Pasternak, and Victor Shklovsky. Yet, in 1937, his reputation as one of the best Russian émigréwriters firmly established, he again had to bolt, this time to elude the growing Nazi threat in Germany (his wife, Véra, was Jewish). He settled in France for three years, departing only three weeks before his apartment was destroyed by bombs as German tanks thundered into Paris. Along with Einstein, Thomas and Heinrich Mann, Brecht, Bartók, Chagall, and a host of other thinkers, authors, musicians, and painters, Nabokov escaped Hitler's Europe for the sanctuary of the United States. In 1945, as World War II drew to a close, he became an American citizen, delighting in what he saw as America's diversity, freedom, and richly textured culture, even though he had to begin to win recognition for himself as a writer all over again in a new language and in midcareer.

The period during which he wrote *Lolita* (1951–53) and during which the novel first appeared in Paris and slowly began its ascent toward its status as an American icon (1955–59) saw change whirl across the national and international landscape. The decade opened with the Korean War (1950–53) and saw Dwight D. Eisenhower's drab presidency (1953–61), as well as the death of the Soviet Union's totalitarian leader Josef Stalin (1953). In Cuba, Fidel Castro commenced his guerrilla attacks on Fulgencio Batista, which culminated in 1959 in the dictator's overthrow. The Soviet Union launched *Sputnik* in 1957, leading a year later to America's counterlaunch of *Explorer*. While Sen. Joseph McCarthy held his infamous hearings into the possibility of a communist conspiracy, and the word *integration* glossed everyone's lips, Elvis Presley and rock'n'roll, emblems of the antiestablishment, erupted alongside television, a medium that opened up consumer society at the same time it created a pervasive sense of speed, artificiality, and global and intellectual reductionism, challenging the very idea of "reality."

Little wonder that in his study of postwar American fiction Frederick R. Karl cited three key metaphors for the essence of the contradictory 1950s: counterfeiting, invisibility, and being on the road.[1]

Mystery and Minutiae

Taken from William Gaddis's *The Recognitions* (1955), the first points to the gap between the ideal and real in the United States. Taken from Ralph Ellison's *Invisible Man* (1952), the second hints at the forgotten or marginalized portions of the population (African Americans, women, the poor). Taken from Jack Kerouac's *On the Road* (1957), the third refers to the 1950s' quest for an authentic—or, perhaps, simply better—America. From the perspective of much television, a certain innocence and optimism hovered over the country as it drifted into postwar prosperity as a superpower; we need only think, for instance, of the *Leave It to Beaver* series. From the perspective of much fiction and poetry produced during that decade, however, a profound questioning of acceptable modes of literary and social behavior pervaded the fringes of America's psyche. Here we discover Allen Ginsberg's fierce poem "Howl" (1956) and its investigation of homosexuality, alienation, and addiction. We find the loose-knit group of beats, who felt themselves hammered down by the oppressive dominant culture and yet committed (through such aesthetically and politically jarring texts as William Burroughs's *Naked Lunch* [1959]) to explore visionary experience; the role of the artist as prophet, innovator, and outsider; and the genre of autobiography as the only credible literature.

Back for a moment to Nabokov writing poetry as the Bolsheviks stormed the Winter Palace, a potently revealing image of man and writer. While his fiction exhibits superficial similarities to other American literature generated during the 1950s in terms of its interrogation of traditional narrative and social systems, and while *Lolita* often darkly satirizes the bubblegum-chewing brashness of the American consciousness, Nabokov could not have been more different from his contemporaries. A distinguished, trilingual, virtually apolitical Anglophile with stunning hazel eyes, fine brown hair, shabby tweed coats, and a full-voweled Russian version of a Cambridge accent, Nabokov was a playful, coaxing, often gentle, and invariably opinionated professor at Cornell who honestly and openly loved America. In 1965, when President Johnson underwent a gallbladder operation, Nabokov wired him, wishing him a speedy recovery and continued success in his "admirable work" with Vietnam and civil rights legislation. In 1966, Nabokov happily translated Lincoln's Gettysburg Address into Russian when the Library of Congress asked him to do so. And throughout the 1960s he vociferously disapproved of student demonstrations "except in the few countries with real and grim dictatorships."[2]

In short, although *Lolita* had to battle charges of obscenity for more than a decade after its publication and although many of Nabokov's novels explore moral boundaries (pedophilia and murder in *Lolita,* murder in *King, Queen, Knave* [1928], homosexuality and assassination in *Pale Fire* [1962], incest in *Ada* [1969]), Nabokov himself was a happily married man who lived a fairly conservative existence. And, although many of his works explore narrative boundaries (parody and the continually shifting levels of reality and illusion mark his oeuvre), Nabokov hardly looked to the likes of Ginsberg or Burroughs for literary kinship. A master craftsperson, he rejected art that strove toward spontaneity. He adored films, especially the comedy of Buster Keaton, Harold Lloyd, Charlie Chaplin, Laurel and Hardy, and the Marx Brothers, but, most of all, he revered the finely tuned and turned phrase, the sculpted plot intricate as a chess problem. His childhood reading (always in the original) included a grocery list of such authors as Verne, Flaubert, Chekhov, Gogol, Verlaine, Rimbaud, Poe, Conan Doyle, Browning, Kipling, Wells, Conrad, Chesterton, Shakespeare, and Wilde, not to mention such crucial individual texts as Tolstoy's *Anna Karénina* and *War and Peace,* Pushkin's *Eugene Onegin,* and a multivolume German tome on butterflies. By the time he was 12, his father had also introduced him to the work of psychologist and pragmatist William James, whose critical good sense went a long way toward turning the young writer against the myth-making of his lifelong intellectual bêtes noires, Freud and Marx.

As an adult, he considered the four greatest novels of the twentieth century Franz Kafka's *Metamorphosis,* Andrey Bely's *Petersburg,* James Joyce's *Ulysses,* and Marcel Proust's *Remembrance of Things Past.* He twice read all 12 volumes of the latter, and perhaps Proust's magnum opus went farther than any of the other books on his short list toward reinforcing his literary and philosophical predilections in *Lolita.* Lo and Humbert's relationship parallels Albertine and Marcel's in Proust's work: both Lolita and Albertine are held prisoner, both Marcel and Humbert (both given to frequent fits of jealousy) are in a sense seduced. More important, though, is that the power of memory is prime in both novels, as is the obsession with time itself. Humans, both books contend, cannot hold onto the past they have lived through. Only through memory and its accomplice, imagination, can characters like Marcel and Humbert deal with the powerful and shifting pain of loss.

Yet, despite Nabokov's voluminous reading, even throughout his last years (spent in the elegant Montreux Palace Hotel in Switzerland), he maintained that he had been influenced by no writer. Why? Because he detested being part of any group, being labeled, endorsing any abstraction. He was the kind of man who ardently believed in democracy, yet never voted; who was utterly uninterested in organized religion in any form, yet was convinced that something existed beyond the merely material. He eschewed political debate and the syllogistic argument his father (scholar of criminal law, politician, and political journalist) practiced with ease, because Nabokov held that while logic had its place, it could never reveal the lush multidimensional truth of things. He called Freud, with his grandiose theories, a witchdoctor, and he denigrated Marx's deductive disposition whenever and wherever he could, choosing rather to celebrate inductively the mystery and minutiae of the natural world, the unpredictable particulars that form each of us, the idea of difference. For Nabokov, consciousness was a space of freedom, not determinism, and art was that gesture which breaks our familiar perceptions, pierces facile generalizations, and makes us see ourselves and our surroundings every second as if for the first time.

2

Waking Us in the Midst of Our Dreaming

Lolita is Nabokov's most famous, infamous, and widely translated novel, spawning as it has Turkish, Bengali, Malayalam, Arabic, braille, and even pirated Chinese editions, to name but a few. Remarkably, however, it was never nominated for a National Book Award, even though five other Nabokov books were.[1] And, more remarkably, Nabokov never received the Nobel Prize for his impressive achievements, even though his name was mentioned in connection with it from the beginning of the 1960s until his death in 1977 and even though we might take some slight solace in the fact that many of the most influential fiction writers of the twentieth century—Kafka, Proust, Joyce, Borges, and Pynchon, among them—never received it either. Not that other major authors did not comprehend Nabokov's importance to the world of literature: when his fellow Russian, Solzhenitsyn, won the prize in 1970, he claimed Nabokov deserved the honor more than he did, and went on to nominate him for it—to, of course, no avail.

Nonetheless, we still read Nabokov, and in great numbers, especially that work of his which lent new meaning to the word *nymphet*. Why? In these politically sensitive and theoretically skeptical times, it is an iffy if not perilous move to talk of such things as "masterworks" and "greatness." Partially this is because such notions now smack of elitism and exclusivity, partially because we have only recently come to understand just how culturally and temporally relative such notions actually are. These difficulties are compounded when discussing *Lolita* because it has only accumulated less than half a century of literary life, a pittance compared with the resilience of an *Odyssey* or *Hamlet*. So perhaps the best we can do, perhaps the best we can ever do, is assert that here, now, *Lolita* captures the heart and imagination of a large well-read segment of our society.

What might account for the novel's capacity to do so is its impulse to wake us in the midst of our dreaming, to defamiliarize the cosmos around us, as the Russian formalists said, so that we now view it afresh.[2] In a revealingly sharp-tongued review in the *New York Times Book Review* of Jean-Paul Sartre's novel *Nausea* (24 April 1949), Nabokov took the existentialist thinker to task for embracing "a fashionable brand of café philosophy" and "inflict[ing] his idle and arbitrary philosophic fancy on a helpless person whom he has invented for that purpose." An exam question from Nabokov's European fiction course at Cornell reads, "Describe Emma [Bovary's] eyes, hands, sunshade, hairdo, dress, shoes" (Boyd 1991, 187). Nabokov, that is, despised abstractions while reveling in the unexpected, in individual freedom, in the item itself. Akin to William Carlos Williams in this respect, if not in others, he believed there were no ideas but in things. Filled with grateful awe before the complexity of existence, the presence of the extraordinary within the ordinary, he intuited that to the extent we accept prefabricated ideas and emotions, the general over the specific, the generic over the original, we exist in a perpetual perceptual and conceptual stupor.

His impulse to rouse us from this manifests itself in various ways in *Lolita*. First, the book urges us to reexperience the beauty and intricacy of expression. As Nabokov commented in his 1956 afterword to the book, *Lolita* is not so much a love affair with the romantic novel as it is with the English language (316). His is a book as much about words as about wicked Humbert, abused Lolita, the force of desire. It is about the joy of sounds: "Lolita, light of my life, fire of my loins. My sin, my soul. Lo-lee-ta: the tip of the tongue taking a trip of three steps down the palate to tap, at three, on the teeth. Lo. Lee. Ta" (9). Closer to the passionate intensity of lyric poetry than the linear language of traditional fiction, such a passage is pure Nabokov in its massive use of alliteration, assonance, and word repetition; its lilting rhythms; its neoclassically sculpted prose; its slightly out-of-the-ordinary diction and startling metaphor; its strong flavor of foreshadowing (its fervor humorously looks ahead to the burning of Humbert's dyspepsia during the seduction scene at the Enchanted Hunters); literary allusiveness (the mention of fiery loins, sinfulness, and spirituality hearkens back to St. Augustine's *Confessions,* while the "lee" in "Lo-lee-ta" conjures up Poe's poem "Annabel Lee" as well as the Annabel Leigh in Nabokov's text whom Humbert blames for his obsessions); and its eye for detail (if we say Lo's name as Humbert prompts, we realize the caress of the Spanish or Italian pronunciation is preferable to the harsh, heavy *L* and wide, crass *O* of the American).

Added to this, we discover if we read on another page or two, are Nabokov's vast lexical range, signature puns, comic etymologies, funny rhymes, double entendres, French phrases, precise sense of colors, and relish for esoteric and portmanteau words. Humbert Humbert's language, like Humbert himself, flaunts a zest for excess, yet its reward is the antimatter of pornography's clumsy prose and cheap linguistic thrills (here it a behooves us to remember not a single obscenity surfaces in Nabokov's published works). Unlike such minimalists as Hemingway and Raymond Carver, with their finely clipped, fast, and predictable sentences, Nabokov was a maximalist possessing a poet's ear for language, an artist's eye for shape and tint, and a lepidopterist's passion for the particular. His is a prose of surprise. It is impossible to second-guess where one of his sentences will head, and as in Shakespeare, his verbal astonishments continually delight us.

Lolita, lest we forget, is also downright funny. We frequently find ourselves laughing aloud at the author's black humor and Humbert's brilliant barbs, his devious parody of Eliot's "Ash Wednesday," his grotesque description of Gaston Godin ("a flabby, dough-faced, melancholy bachelor tapering upward to a pair of narrow, not quite level shoulders and a conical pear-shaped head which has sleek black hair on one side and only a few plastered wisps on the other" [181]), his linguistically slapstick death struggle with Quilty ("I rolled over him. We rolled over me. They rolled over him. We rolled over us" [299]). Often such black humor slides into satire, humor with a moral purpose, as Humbert and Nabokov bitingly delineate the American landscape of the 1950s, where Dairy Queen fades to "Frigid Queen," Disneyland "umber and black Humberland" (166).

This last point indicates another reason *Lolita* is significant. It documents the United States in two important ways: first, by snapping a meticulously detailed photo of the country at a certain moment in its history; and, second, through the postpublication obscenity controversy it generated, by helping illuminate the country's conception of art. In both ways, it makes us re-view America.

It also makes us re-view ourselves, rethink our beliefs, as it raises a number of intriguing questions. Is *Lolita* a principled book, a sexist one, an affirmation of transcendent love, of debauchery, of art? Should we feel sympathy, pity, fear, or all three for Humbert? For Lolita? What is Nabokov's attitude toward him, her? Toward America? Toward Europe? What sort of universe does Nabokov propose we live in? What are we to make of all those metafictional games played in a novel that ostensibly deals with such deadly serious subjects as child molestation and homicide? What, ultimately, is the *point* of *Lolita*? Readers feel, after the fact, that they have never quite finished reading or interpreting a book as emotionally complicated, stunningly well-crafted, multidimensionally resonant, humanly humorous, psychologically haunting, and historically rich as *Lolita*. In its paradoxical exploration of the bright and dark sides of what it means to be a man or woman, it continues to invite us back into its moving intricacies again and again, each time providing us with new insights into the geography of its internal structure and ours, and, if such matters do not finally make a text vital and momentous, even great, here and now, it is hard to know exactly what does.

3

Hurricane Lolita

Nabokov is one of the most studied postwar authors, his work having begot nearly 50 scholarly books and volumes of collected essays, tens of unpublished dissertations, hundreds of articles, and nigh countless reviews. A fruitful year of inquiry into his oeuvre can witness the appearance of nearly 70 pieces of criticism. During 1974 alone, a particularly rich 12 months of investigation, no fewer than 7 books, 5 dissertations, and 56 chapters or articles touching on him appeared in print. Of those, at least 5 monographs, a dissertation, and a baker's dozen of articles focused directly on *Lolita*—a sum that underscores that text's status as one of the most studied postwar novels.

But it was a tough one for Nabokov to write and an even tougher one for him to get published. First, he felt a tremendous emotional distance from his protagonist, Humbert Humbert. Always fascinated by the perverse (as long as it was held at arm's length), Nabokov nonetheless was an almost blandly psychologically normal man himself and one who found it a formidable challenge to inhabit and shape the consciousness of a liar, cheat, pedophile, rapist, and killer. In 1950 he nearly incinerated what he had amassed of the book, and probably would have succeeded, had not his wife, Véra, prevailed on him not to give up.

Composing *Lolita* was also arduous in the sense that it took decades for it to coalesce in Nabokov's imagination. Usually, a new novel would flash upon him more or less complete. He would then mull over each detail in it for quite a while—frequently half a year or so—before finally beginning to transcribe it quickly. *Lolita*, however, strained to be born from the late 1930s onward. As early as *Laughter in the Dark* (1932), an Ur-*Lolita* surfaces when Albinus Kretschmar sacrifices everything for a girl whom he loses to a hack artist named Axel Rex. Five years later, in *The Gift,* a character offhandedly tells a "Dostoevskian" story in which an old man falls in love with a young girl who does not return his affections and then marries her widowed mother to be near his idol. In 1939, in an even more *Lolita*-esque tale entitled "Volshebnik," or "The Enchanter," a 49-year-old Central European named Arthur weds a rich French widow in order to be near her 12-year-old daughter. When the widow dies, Arthur sets out on vacation with the girl. During his first night alone with her in a hotel room, he fondles what he believes to be her sleeping body, only to discover that she is in reality wide awake and staring up at him in horror. Shocked and riddled with guilt, he flees the building and throws himself under a truck in the street below. Written from a distant third-person point of view, and unfulfillingly sketchy, the 54-page typescript of "The Enchanter" remained undiscovered among Nabokov's papers until 1964 and untranslated and unpublished until 1986, nine years after his death.

Nevertheless, as early as 1946 he began contemplating turning "The Enchanter" into a novel. He originally thought to title it *The Kingdom by the Sea*, after the line in Poe's "Annabel Lee" (1849), a poem dealing with the deep doomed love between two children, or *Ginny*, after Virginia Clemm, Poe's 13-year-old cousin whom the 27-year-old writer married in 1836. By 1951, Nabokov, now an associate professor at Cornell, had started composing the book in earnest. Always a scholar-scientist with a keen eye for the specific and an encyclopedic mind (Alfred Appel, Jr., recalls that, in the course of one typical two-hour conversation with Nabokov, the author touched on no fewer than 20 subjects, from *Li'l Abner* to medieval art, bird life on Lake Geneva to Lenny Bruce, John Updike's work to the kind of beetle into which Gregor Samsa finds himself transformed in Kafka's *Metamorphosis*), he researched his work-in-progress by reading newspaper articles on pedophilia and gruesome murderers, case studies about child molesters, gun histories, teen magazines, Girl Scout manuals, home decorating guides, and pieces on barbiturates and the Lascaux cave paintings. He even traveled on school buses to listen to how American teenage girls actually spoke. During this period his summertime lepping sojourns also took him to more than 200 motels in 46 states on all the roads traversed by Humbert and his nymphet. Because by this stage in the novel's development he could finally visualize his project in toto, he drafted whatever section he fancied at the moment, penning out of chronological sequence, putting together Humbert's diary first, then Humbert and Lolita's trip west, Quilty's murder, Humbert's earlier life, and eventually the remainder of the action—all the while using index cards, which he had grown accustomed to employing from his lepidopteralogical research.

And yet, interestingly, this was not his sole pursuit during the early 1950s. Far from it. While working on *Lolita*, Nabokov also had his fingers in many other creative and cerebral pies, spending 6 hours a week delivering lectures at Cornell, 2 leading a seminar, 18 prepping and grading, 30 researching (not only *Lolita*, but also his monumental study of *Eugene Onegin*), and 35 writing (usually in the evenings, sometimes through the night, and, again, not only *Lolita* but also *Conclusive Evidence* and then *Pnin*). Even with this brain-numbing schedule, he finished his twelfth book in fewer than five years.

On its completion, though, Nabokov was confronted by a fresh set of problems. American publishers, worried about fines and imprisonment if *Lolita* were found obscene by the courts, repeatedly turned down the manuscript, which for a short while Nabokov thought about publishing anonymously (a choice that, in retrospect, would have almost surely made matters worse). Simon and Schuster rejected it on the grounds that it was pornographic, and Viking Press, the *New Yorker*, New Directions, Farrar Straus, Doubleday, and one or two European venues followed suit. The literary agent Madame Ergaz of the Bureau Littéraire Clairovin in Paris then submitted it to Maurice Girodias's Olympia Press. While it is true that Girodias's list included or would soon include such superbly talented avant-garde writers as Samuel Beckett, Henry Miller, and William Burroughs, it is equally true that three-fourths of it flaunted works with titles like *Until She Screams* and *The Sexual Life of Robinson Crusoe*. Apparently unaware of such matters, Nabokov signed a contract with Girodias on 6 June 1955. In October the final product turned up in Nabokov's mailbox: two rather seedily pale olive-green paperback volumes in the Olympia Traveller's Companion series, part of a 5,000-copy print run.

All the rest—or so it seemed initially—was silence. For obvious reasons, no reviews emerged and virtually no one took notice of the book. No one, that is, until early the following year when out of the blue Graham Greene in England recommended *Lolita* as one of the best novels of 1955, a suggestion immediately attacked by a columnist in the *Sunday Express*. This attack prompted Greene to reply in the *Spectator*, in turn prompting Harvey Breit to allude to the exchange in the *New York Times Book Review* (26 February 1956) and then, two weeks later, devote two-thirds of a column to it. Such an electric debate jump-started the American literary engine, and publicity for Nabokov's book continued to swell when U.S. Customs briefly seized an Olympia Press copy of it in June. Howard Nemerov wrote an angry letter to the *New York Times* (30 October 1956) comparing the novel with *Ulysses* and declaring that "by the mere corruption of taste, and by the ample provision of substitutes for literature, our society is already so well protected against good writing that Mr. Nabokov's book might be allowed to enter the United States without occasioning the fear of any general deterioration of morals or improvement of minds." The next year, in New York, the *Anchor Review* devoted 112 pages to Nabokov, including a long excerpt from *Lolita* as well as its afterword, and in June, R. W. Flint reviewed this offering in the *New Republic*, delighting in the writer's language, his rich narrative surprises, and his ribald burlesque of Freudianism, and concluding that the appearance of these excerpts amounted to a major literary event in the

United States. The publishing road now paved, Putnam brought out the $5 American version on Monday, 18 August 1958.

In a diary kept especially for documenting this exceptional stage in his career, Nabokov referred to what occurred next as "Hurricane Lolita." Things moved extraordinarily quickly and extraordinarily dramatically. To say that *Lolita* made a cultural splash is to understate the case considerably. Within four days of its American publication, it had gone into its third printing. Within three weeks it had sold 100,000 copies. It jetted to the top of the *New York Times* best-seller list, where it hovered for nearly a year. And, by late 1958, it had become part of the American consciousness, news of its "scandalous" existence disseminated on the television through jokes by Steve Allen, Dean Martin, and Milton Berle. ("I've put off reading *Lolita* for six years," Groucho Marx quipped one evening, "till she's 18" [Boyd 1991, 376].)

Even though Nabokov was soon to vacate his teaching post at Cornell and even though there seemed to be a good deal of jealousy among his colleagues concerning this antisocial and constitutionally detached author's rapid success (he never graced a single faculty meeting with his presence), a cult sprang up around him on campus among students, comprising such future literati as editor C. Michael Curtis, critic Roger Sale, and writers Richard Fariña, Steve Katz, Thomas Pynchon, and Joanna Russ. Fawcett Crest bought the paperback rights for $100,000 and Harris-Kubrick Pictures the movie rights for $150,000 plus 15 percent of the producer's profits. Nabokov was paid $40,000 (as well as transportation to and from Los Angeles, and expenses) to write the screenplay and another $35,000 if he received sole credit for it. Meanwhile, controversy about the novel that would be translated into more than 25 languages erupted around the globe. The Cincinnati Public Library, among many others, barred the novel from its shelves in September 1958, while *Lolita* sold out on publication day in England a year later, created massive controversy in Italy, and was banned in such diverse countries as France (on three separate occasions), Belgium, Australia, New Zealand, South Africa, and Burma, the Swedish version not quieting the hubbub any when it highlighted the erotic passages and cut much of the rest of the text.

Nabokov's reaction to all this? He felt it all should have happened to him 30 years earlier. Ever since self-publishing his first collection of poems in 1916 and subsequently hearing from a literary friend of his father that he would never be a writer, Nabokov was fairly indifferent to reviews of his work. He knew what he was up to, and he was understandably confident about his impressive gifts. But a quick glance at the early appraisals of *Lolita* is instructive because they raise a cluster of interpretive questions that have to a great extent preoccupied Nabokov critics and general readers in one way or another for more than four decades. Is *Lolita* pornographic, immoral, obscene? Why? Why not? And, if so, is it ethical to write such a thing, to publish it, to read it? Is it a love story? Can a story of nympholepsy be about love? In what sense? Is Humbert Humbert evil, insane, perverted, sympathetic, understandable, romantic, reliable, an artist, something else? What, precisely, are his crimes? What made him the way he is? And what about Lolita? How are we as readers supposed to feel toward her? Do we know anything about her except what Humbert wants us to know? Is there anything else to know? Why did Humbert write his book? Why did Nabokov write his? What should we make of all the game-playing, from allusions to puns, burlesques to parodies, mirrors to McFate, coincidence to clearly guilty Clare Quilty? How can we read this text as a comment on the role of creator in our society? The creative process itself? American culture? The 1950s? Freudianism? Marxism? Freedom and free will? What it means, finally, to be a human in the second half of the twentieth century?

The first full review of *Lolita* was written by John Hollander in the fall 1956 issue of the intellectually rigorous *Partisan Review*. It set the tone for many of the cheerful ones that followed by relishing the novel's dark humor both at the level of language and situation, asserting that *Lolita* is not pornographic but parodistic and announcing the book's dominant theme as the impulse to immortalize in art that which is all too ephemeral in life. Other enthusiastic reviews along the same lines were published in such major and wide-ranging newspapers and magazines as *Commonweal*, *Esquire*, the *New Yorker*, the *San Francisco Chronicle*, the *Saturday Review*, and *Time*. Elizabeth Janeway's in the *New York Times Book Review*, printed the day before

Lolita's American debut and igniting a number of passionate letters to the editor, chimed in with these but also sensitively argued that below the splendid humor found by Hollander and others darts an unutterable sadness generated by a book in which a fairy tale devolves into a nightmare. Humbert is an Everyman "driven by desire, wanting his Lolita so badly that it never occurs to him to consider her as a human being." Janeway concluded with the comment that no book "is more likely to quench the flames of lust than this exact and immediate description of its consequences."

Many readers took exception. While roughly two-thirds of the pioneer reviews were positive, at least one-third covered the gamut from simply unimpressed to downright nasty. Fanning the controversy (and the sales), a number of periodicals, the *New Republic* and the *New York Times* among them, published both positive and negative takes on Nabokov's novel. Robert Hatch in the *Nation* (23 June 1962) felt *Lolita* was "not a very inventive book—beyond the initial audacity," and Granville Hicks in the *Saturday Review* (16 August 1958) considered it "not one of the more memorable novels."

Indicative of even less flattering assessments was John Gordon's piece in the tabloidish British *Sunday Express* (29 January 1956), which lambasted *Lolita* for being "the filthiest book I have ever read," not to mention "sheer unrestrained pornography." Near to this in flavor was Harold C. Gardiner's piece in *America* (30 August 1958); he both attacked other critics for employing mental and moral gymnastics to get around *Lolita*'s decadence and called the book "the most obscene lubrication to disgrace U.S. publishing in many a decade." On the heels of this came Orville Prescott's evaluation in the *New York Times* on the day of *Lolita*'s American publication. Prescott held that "there are two equally serious reasons why [*Lolita*] isn't worth any adult reader's attention. The first is that it is dull, dull, dull in a pretentious, florid and archly fatuous fashion. The second is that it is repulsive." This was seconded by Riley Hughes in *Catholic World* (October 1958). He wrote that the "very subject matter makes [*Lolita*] a book to which grave objection must be raised. . . . As a study of unnatural infatuation, of a man and mind obsessed, it might be said to have a certain clinical authority. But the aura of evil, the implications of a decadence universally accepted and shared—this is a romp which does not amuse." In England, Kingsley Amis (*Spectator*, 6 November 1959) was even less charitable. For him, *Lolita* was a plainly bad book, both morally and artistically: overpraised, overwritten, and unredeemingly degenerate.

Regardless of such brutal judgments (or perhaps to some degree because of them), interest in *Lolita* by general readers and scholars alike deepened over the next few years. During the late 1950s and early 1960s, essays like the one by F. W. Dupee in *Encounter* (February 1959) began to cast a backward glance in an attempt to document and make sense of *Lolita*'s rocky publishing history. Others undertook the first influence studies, listening to the book for reverberations of Rabelais's rhapsodic fantasies, Laclos's psychosexual intrigues in *Les Liaisons dangereuses*, Swift's dark satire, Poe's tales of ratiocination and love affair with Virginia Clemm, Dostoevsky's spiritual quest in *Crime and Punishment*, Proust's attempt to capture time in art in *Remembrance of Things Past*, and Kerouac's American cross-country odyssey in *On the Road*. Diana Butler uncovered the guiding butterfly metaphor in her seminal 1960 essay "*Lolita* Lepidoptera" (*New World Writing* 16), while still others explored the book's self-conscious sabotage of the traditional love story, its use of comedy as an existential affirmation of life in a bleak cosmos, and, of course, again, its moral stance, or lack of one.

The first dissertation discussing the book, "Folding the Patterned Carpet: Form and Theme in the Novels of Vladimir Nabokov," completed in 1966 by Susan Fromberg at the University of Chicago, probed the author's need to transcend death by creating patterns that lend meaning to existence. That year also marked the publication of the first and still first-rate book on Nabokov, Page Stegner's *Escape into Aesthetics: The Art of Vladimir Nabokov*, which outlined a number of key motifs in Nabokov's English works, including anti-Freudianism, the unreality of time and space, the relationship between illusion and reality, verbal play, and the parody of conventional literary forms. According to Stegner, *Lolita* is Nabokov's greatest novel, a book that affects readers in many different ways on many different levels that move light-years beyond mere questions of obscenity or puzzles planted in its narrative structure: it asks us for a compassionate understanding of Humbert's suffering.

Stegner's book was followed in 1967 by the first issue of a scholarly journal dedicated exclusively to Nabokov, the spring *Wisconsin Studies in Contemporary Literature*, edited by L. S. Dembo, which included a fine piece on the self-reflexive nature of *Lolita* by Alfred Appel, Jr., and a select bibliography of criticism through 1966 by Jackson R. Bryer and Thomas J. Bergin, Jr. Of yet more significance that year was the publication of Andrew Field's important, if sometimes inaccurate, *Nabokov: His Life and Art*. Even today probably the best-known critical study of the author, Field's book was not only the first to elucidate and unify Nabokov's Russian and English fictions but also the first to raise the writer's overall project to primary scholarly concern. While he would go on to compile a Nabokov bibliography (1973) and two flawed biographies (1977, 1986), Field's first book on Nabokov concentrated on a survey of the author's works. In his chapter on *Lolita*, he contended that by killing Quilty, Humbert kills his own dark side and thereby transforms his object of perverse passion into one of love. Essentially a psychological reading, this chapter also touched on Proust's presence as well as the pivotal metaphors of prison and chess in the text.

The 1960s drew to a close with the publication of Carl Proffer's *Keys to Lolita* (1968), the first exquisitely detailed exegesis of Nabokov's novel, with investigations of its literary allusions, clues leading to Quilty's identity, and stylistic devices, while the 1970s commenced with two other considerable occurrences in Nabokov criticism. First was the publication of the splendid *The Annotated Lolita* (1970) by Alfred Appel, Jr., replete with a laudable 67-page introduction, the painstakingly edited text of the novel itself, and 121 pages of notes tracing a wealth of allusions, principal motifs, and themes. Second was the publication of the winter 1970 issue of *TriQuarterly*, subsequently reprinted as *Nabokov: Criticism, Reminiscences, Translations, and Tributes*, edited as a belated seventieth-birthday present to the writer by Alfred Appel, Jr. and Charles Newman, with contributions by John Barth, Anthony Burgess, R. H. W. Dillard, John Updike, Alfred Kazin, and more than 40 other important writers and critics that further solidified Nabokov's position as a major force in the universe of contemporary letters, one who John Leonard once bemusedly dubbed "the Nobel-ist writer of them all" (*New York Times*, 1 May 1969).

These publications were soon complemented by the first book-length introductions to Nabokov aimed at a general readership: Julian Moynahan's study (1971), part of the University of Minnesota's Pamphlets on Writers Series, which briefly placed *Lolita* in the tradition of fiction dealing with the quest for the American dream; Donald E. Morton's (1974), part of Fredrick Ungar's Modern Literature Monographs Series, which held that *Lolita* is about the role of the imagination in the struggle between life and fate; and L. L. Lee's (1976), part of Twayne's United States Authors Series, which affirmed a moral reading of the text while simultaneously touching on its American elements, important allusions, and exploration of Humbert's and Lolita's attempts to escape the cage of everyday reality.

By the twentieth anniversary of its original publication, *Lolita* had firmly taken its place in the literary canon. Losing interest in questions concerning the novel's obscenity, and recently falling under sway of structuralism and the first birth pangs of poststructuralism, critics began to focus ever more attention on the book's self-conscious heart and bright narrative tactics. Julia Bader, for instance, in *Crystal Land: Artifice in Nabokov's English Novels* (1972), argued that through *Lolita*'s parodic style, lovemaking is equated with literary technique, and Elizabeth W. Bruss, in her chapter on *Lolita* in *Autobiographical Acts: The Changing Situation of a Literary Genre* (1976), contended that Nabokov's novel is a burlesque of autobiography wherein Humbert, continually shifting genres as he writes, ultimately comes to understand the unreality of the autobiographical act. Other typical examples of such approaches include those by Maurice Couturier, who, while talking at length about sexuality in *Lolita* in his 1979 analysis, nonetheless heavily foregrounded the novel's poetics, and by Nomi Tamir-Ghez, who examined Humbert's rhetorical strategies in her extremely perceptive "The Art of Persuasion in Nabokov's *Lolita*" (*Poetics Today*, 1979). Meanwhile, Samuel Schuman brought out the first extensive annotated bibliography of Nabokov criticism from 1931 to 1977, strengthening the roots of Nabokov studies, while the *Vladimir Nabokov Research Newsletter*, the first scholarly periodical dedicated to the author, appeared, running until 1984 when it became the *Nabokovian*.

Curiously, almost at the very moment *Lolita* settled comfortably into the literary canon, a certain disinterest with it and its author developed on the part of general readers. By the year the man who created Dolly Haze died (and in spite of the fact that such writers as Solzhenitsyn, Robbe-Grillet, and Anthony Burgess acclaimed him a genius), J. D. O'Hara could comment that Nabokov occupied "a strange position in the Alps of contemporary literature, at once admired and forgotten" (*Canto*, Spring 1977). Admired by the critics, forgotten by the rest: why? For one thing, American culture itself had changed, and changed dramatically. At a time when *Deep Throat* and *The Texas Chainsaw Massacre* could be seen at the local cinema and soon, through the magic of the video, rented for viewing in the privacy of one's own living room, *Lolita*'s initial audacity began to pale. Indeed, before too long the novel began to feel downright tame. Given the new social context in which it existed, questions concerning its obscenity came to seem quaint and then slight. Next, *Lolita* had entered the canon, which is to say it began to be taught and taught frequently in colleges. It became required reading. This eventuality surely led some students to wonder just how interesting such a text could really be, tainted as it was by the dusty film of the academy. Moreover, it appears that *Ada*, published in 1969 to a constellation of superlative reviews by the likes of Alfred Appel, Jr., and Alfred Kazin, and reaching the front page of the *New York Times Book Review* and the front cover of *Time*, sparked a negative reaction to its writer among general readers for its deliberately unwieldy and often seemingly unintelligible massiveness. Enough, people believed, was enough. Moreover, 29 volumes of Nabokov's work had seen print in English in a relatively short 14 years. A kind of critical saturation point was reached. On top of this, his last two novels, *Transparent Things* (1972) and *Look at the Harlequins!* (1974), received mixed reviews, while his publisher, McGraw-Hill, began to show less interest in him as it shied farther and farther away from fiction. Last, the critical climate in America and abroad had shifted as well:

> With the rise of feminism, novelists like Doris Lessing and Margaret Atwood aroused excited attention. Someone so decidedly male as Nabokov, equipped by his upbringing with gentlemanly notions of honor and more comfortable with woman as muse than woman as writer, seemed a relic of the past. After all, it was he who had created Humbert, for whom Lolita barely exists except as a mere object of *his* emotion and *his* imagination. It could be easily overlooked that for Nabokov Lolita was quite a different creature, a person in her own right, and one of the characters he found most admirable in all his works, or that his book seethed with indignation of Humbert's manipulation of *all* the women in his life. (Boyd 1991, 655)

Despite such public disinterest and the hint of critical acrimony, and fueled both by recent theoretical developments and a very real need to reappraise Nabokov's accomplishments, scholars once more turned their attention to the writer's work in general and *Lolita* in particular. The results during the 1980s and early 1990s proved abundant, diverse, and exhilarating. Indicative is David Packman's intriguing poststructuralist inquiry, *Vladimir Nabokov: The Structure of Literary Desire* (1982), which maintained that *Lolita* plays and replays with the detective genre by transforming both Humbert Humbert and the reader into sleuths in a highly self-reflexive linguistic configuration while concurrently doubling Humbert Humbert's desire in the text with the reader's desire to know what happens next. Along similarly innovative lines is Thomas R. Frosch's essay "Parody and Authenticity in *Lolita*" (1982) and its proposal that Nabokov's novel participates in a form of "metaparody" that attempts to transcend mere allusions to, and fun-poking at, other works and to travel toward bona fide originality.

Meanwhile, looking at the book from a sociohistorical point of view in his chapter on John Hawkes and Nabokov in *American Fictions: 1940–1980* (1983), Frederick R. Karl contextualized *Lolita* as a celebration of the counterfeit in American culture during the 1950s. David Rampton, in *Vladimir Nabokov: A Critical Study of the Novels* (1984), argued against critics who privileged aesthetic over moral concerns in *Lolita*, thereby launching what would prove to be a succession of humanist reevaluations of Nabokov's project. Rampton's undertaking was endorsed in 1989 by Leona Toker in *Nabokov: The Mystery of Literary Structures*, which examined the moral significance of the rhetoric of reader entrapment in *Lolita*, and in 1992 (33 years after his father's attack on the book) by Martin Amis in his thoughtful layreader's article "*Lolita* Reconsidered," appearing in the *Atlantic* and in many ways reintroducing Nabokov's novel to the American reading public. Editors such as Norman Page (1982), Phyllis A. Roth (1984), and Harold Bloom (1987) collected some of the finest essays and reviews about Nabokov and his most widely recognized and read text. Michael Juliar, in *Vladimir Nabokov: A Descriptive Bibliography* (1986), amassed the most complete bibliography of the author's writings to date. Psychoanalytic critics such as Geoffrey Green, in his *Freud and Nabokov* (1988), deliberately began to read against the novelist's antagonism toward that "Austrian crank with a shabby umbrella."[1] And theophilosophical readers such as Vladimir E. Alexandrov, in *Nabokov's Otherworlds* (1991), began to probe the presence of an occult or spiritual dimension in Nabokov's universe.

From a certain perspective, the capstone of much of this labor was Brian Boyd's superb, colossal, double-volumed critical biography, *Vladimir Nabokov: The Russian Years* (1990) and *Vladimir Nabokov: The American Years* (1991). Therein he righted several wrongs about the author's life generated by Field in his faulty early work, compiled much new information about Nabokov and his world, and provided close careful readings of all his texts, including an exploration of *Lolita* that once again reemphasized its moral compass. Such vital probes went a very good distance toward reinvigorating Nabokov studies at the turn of the millennium.

But what will future critics have to say about the novel Nabokov held as his "special favorite" (*SO*, 15)? Traditional investigations revealing and reevaluating new and old influences, themes, and leitmotifs will surely continue to see the light of publication, as will meticulous bibliographic surveys and compilations into easily available volumes of excellent previously published essays and book chapters. In addition, a fair number of analyses, influenced by the rapid proliferation of critical theory in America and abroad during the late 1970s and 1980s, will continue (or in some cases only now begin) to view the novel through more deliberately theoretical eyes. Much work remains to be done, for instance, from feminist perspectives investigating the role of women in this work, women's responses to it, the complexity of gender issues manifested in its pages, and its relationship to Nabokov's entire oeuvre. Little has been written about such reader-response concerns as how we go about making sense of this text, how we experience it as a growing process of anticipation, frustration, retrospection, and reconstruction. Even less has been written about such deconstructive ones as the text's dismantling of determinate meaning, its self-questioning, and its potentially infinite deferment of truth, or such Marxist and more generally sociohistorical ones as the way economic, class, and ideological determinants perform within it.

Yet the critics who do undertake such reenergizing interpretive strategies will be well served by remembering Nabokov's own deep suspicion of closed (and hence deadening) systems. They will be well served, too, by recalling those early oxymoronic assaults on him for being both too cerebral and too sensual, too neoclassical and too romantic, too complex and too obvious, too depressing and too witty, too immoral and too didactic. If we have learned anything over the past four decades or so about Nabokov's and *Lolita*'s critical reception, it has been that these assaults have ultimately accomplished little except to affirm Nabokov's breadth of mind and feeling, his enduring literary skill and very human wisdom, and his intellectual and emotional impact on an entire culture.

A READING

4

The Moral Dimension:
Umber and Black Humberland

THE PROMISE OF PORN

Lolita, it would seem, is ubiquitous in our world, from John Fowles's novel *The Collector* (1963), about a young woman's ordeal as the prisoner of a psychopath with a passion for butterflies, to the conclusion of Don DeLillo's *White Noise* (1985), in which the protagonist's comic shooting of his adversarial double darkly echoes Humbert's of Quilty. From Alan Jay Lerner and John Barry's 1971 musical version of Nabokov's bestseller (starring John Neville and Annette Ferra), which flopped during out-of-town tryouts, to Edward Albee's stage adaptation (starring Donald Sutherland and Blanche Baker), which opened on 28 March 1981 and closed after 12 performances. From songs such as The Police's 1980 hit "Don't Stand So Close to Me," chronicling an older teacher's desire for one of his younger students (the song mentions the novel by name), to the headlines, books, made-for-television movies, and even comics of the early 1990s about Amy Fisher, the celebrity teen felon referred to by the media as "the Long Island Lolita," who gunned down her older lover's wife. And even to *Ekaterina,* Donald Harington's funny if flawed 1993 novel, deeply indebted to Nabokov's 1955 *Lolita,* about the life of one Vladimirovna Dadeshkeliani, an exiled Russian princess with a fetish for "faunlets," the male counterparts of Humbert's nymphets.

Lolita, with its murder, pedophilia, sadism, masochism, and even hint of incest, clearly struck a nerve in our society by violating a number of its strongest taboos. Over the years, Nabokov's novel has come to represent nothing less than obscenity itself in the minds of many people, and yet it has frequently been judged and juried without the benefit of having had its covers cracked open. Through a series of media hyperboles and critical mirroring distortions, it has developed in our culture's consciousness into an icon for the idea of transgression. As with much literature written using fantastic tint (we need only recall the various incarnations of the vampire myth with its shadowy sexual connotations, from its early medieval versions, through Bram Stoker's late nineteenth-century *Dracula,* to Anne Rice's late twenti-eth-century *The Vampire Lestat*), *Lolita* seems to present our society with that which it cannot stand: possibilities of radically alternative universes and the limits of civilization itself. The novel thereby appears to question fundamental humanist and religious sanctions concerning what is "proper," "decent," and "acceptable."

It does so in part by promising from its title onward to deliver pure plain pornography. The fictitious John Ray, Jr., reminds us in the first sentence of his fictional foreword that the text we are holding is not simply called *Lolita,* but *Lolita, or the Confession of a White Widowed Male,* a title that hearkens back to such lusty eighteenth-century narratives as John Cleland's *Fanny Hill: Memoirs of a Woman of Pleasure,* not to mention some of the more contemporary ones on Maurice Girodias's Olympia Press book list, which themselves dimly cast a backward glance through carnal-colored glasses to Saint Augustine's fifth-century primo-genitor of the confessional genre, in which he narrates his struggles to free himself from pride and sensuality.

But *Lolita* fails to deliver on its promise. The first 13 chapters of the text, culminating with the oft-cited scene of Lo unwittingly stretching her legs across Humbert's excited lap on the davenport on an iron-ically sunny Sunday morning in June, are the only chapters suggestive of the erotic. And the reader expecting a far dingier book is bound to be disappointed by them. A good emblem for the readerly process, then, is located in the earlier pivotal scene depicting Annabel and Humbert's first failed tryst in the significantly Edenic garden in back of her parents' villa. There Nabokov signals the reader's original frustra-tion as well as Annabel and Humbert's desire for the hard-core. He leads us to the brink of both narrative and sexual gratification only to deny us both. Later Hum leads us through narrative digression after narrative digression on the road to his first tryst with Lolita in a hotel aptly named Enchanted Hunters. Tauntingly, he slows the momentum of his story to a crawl. Meticulous scene replaces speedy summary. He methodically describes the piggish cars parked outside, the piggish people behind the desk, the mirrory room 342, the dining room, the way he coaxes Lo to take the pill he believes will knock her out, the toilet flushings, garbled chatter, falling elevators that sound around him, his excursion into the lobby and onto the white steps beyond while waiting for that magic pill to work, his initial unwitting meeting with Quilty, his return to 342, his slow understanding amid passion and heartburn that his pill and plan have fizzled, his extended medita-tion on longing as the night drags on—and, finally, finally, the deed itself, related thus fleetingly: "by six she was wide awake, and by six fifteen we were technically lovers" (132).

That's it. That's all. Well over 130 pages of painful procrastina-tion and building libido for a fast, diffident 14 words. Adding insult to anticlimactic injury, Humbert informs us two pages on—after again slowing summary into scene, which again leads up to their first tryst only to circumvent its description—that he is "not concerned with so-called 'sex' at all. Anybody can imagine those elements of animality." The unwary reader ready for the real thing is thereby caught in Nabokov's trap, beguiled into believing he or she has just pitched into the pages of a steamy novel only to be implicated as a beast for sharing Humbert's hunger. The closest we come to a graphic depiction of Humbert and Lo's union follows on the heels of this statement. The very next chapter recasts the seduction scene in sexually charged metaphoric terms, a parody of Freudian symbolism, as Hum explains how he would redecorate the murals in the dining room. His additions are replete with lakes, dense arbors, "a tiger pursuing a bird of paradise," "a choking snake sheathing whole the flayed trunk of a shoat," "a callypygean slave child . . . climb[ing] a column of onyx," and "luminous globules of gonadal glow that travel up the opalescent sides of juke boxes" (134). The truth is that we shall never be privy to a peek at Quilty's blue movies made at the mischievously christened Duk Duk (from the Persian slang for *copulation*) Ranch.

Needless to say, those people looking hard enough and reading sloppily enough for something hot here just might be able to find it, despite the exquisitely sculpted prose that gives the lie to porn's clunky prosaism, despite the lack of even one obscene word in the text, and despite the fact that Ray reveals in the second sentence of his prelude that Humbert has died of a coronary thrombosis in jail while awaiting trial—having, that is to say, paid the price even the most emphatic moralist could ever want him to pay for his sins.

In Nabokov's mind, *Lolita* was surely no pornography. And Nabokov himself was surely no Humbert Humbert. On the contrary, as he wrote to his literary sparring partner Edmund Wilson, he thought *Lolita* a "pure and austere work" and "a highly moral affair."[1] In a BBC television interview he went on to say that Lolita had been his "most difficult" novel to write because it explored a subject that was "so distant, so remote, from my own emotional life" (*SO*, 15). That life, according to Nabokov, his friends, and his biographers, was a positively innocuous one. "I pride myself on being a person with no public appeal," he once told several journalists. "I have never been drunk in my life. I never use schoolboy words of four letters. . . . My loathings are simple: stupidity, oppression, crime, cruelty, soft music. My pleasures are the most intense known to man: writing and butterfly hunting" (*SO*, 3). Fred Hills, editor-in-chief at McGraw-Hill, typically found Nabokov "utterly charming, affable, worldly, ready to discuss any subject with ease and pleasure" (Boyd 1991, 645). In reality, and unexpectedly, Nabokov shared many of the conservative views of his early critics with regard to literary sexuality. He believed, for instance, that D. H. Lawrence was little more than a smutty novelist, that Joyce's *Ulysses* had overdone it with respect to the raunchy business, and that "there should certainly be some forms of censorship against commercial pornography."[2]

His loathings, to repeat for emphasis, were simple, and included oppression, crime, and cruelty. That should be a tip-off if ever there was one to Nabokov's aims in *Lolita,* since these base traits amount to Humbert Humbert's modus operandi for much of the novel. He suppresses Lolita's humanity, perpetrates statutory rape and murder, and displays both psychological and physical cruelty to nearly everyone in the text, from his first wife, Valeria, whose breasts he can imagine slapping out of alignment (87), to the psychiatrists he toys with at the sanatorium while recovering from one of his several mental breakdowns (34–35), to four-foot-ten Lolita, into whose hair he sometimes thrusts his fingers "and then gently but firmly clasping them around the nape of her neck . . . lead[s] my reluctant pet to our small home for a quick connection before dinner" (164). That potential for physical violence culminates 63 pages later when, beside himself after finding that Lo has adulterated Quilty's license-plate number on the pad tucked in Humbert's glove compartment, he hauls off and delivers "a tremendous backhand cut that caught her on her hot hard little cheekbone" (227). In many ways, then, Nabokov has made Humbert the Horrible his antithesis, his own dark double, just as Humbert has made Quilty his. "Some of my characters are, no doubt, pretty beastly," Nabokov was quick to point out in a BBC interview, but they exist "outside my inner self like the mournful monsters of a cathedral façade—demons placed there merely to show that they have been booted out" (*SO*, 19). Many early reviewers, some critics, reckless readers, the self-righteously pure, parents with young children, and adults themselves once victims of child abuse have found it exceedingly difficult to traverse the ironic distance between Humbert Humbert's intentions and Nabokov's. Hence they fail to understand, as Boyd accurately observes, that "for Nabokov tenderness and kindness were the essence of art," that he gave us characters like Humbert Humbert "in a spirit of outrage at their travesty of his dearest values" (Boyd 1991, 396).

In light of this, the novel's foreword proves instructive. It is obvious that we should take John Ray's assertions with a shaker of salt. His

Humbertish duplicate cognomen (J.R., Jr.), fluctuating tone, wooden mind (his name conjures up that of the seventeenth-century English naturalist John Ray, known for his rigid systems of classification), and unconscious parody of somber opinions that conventionally preface controversial novels place him firmly among Nabokov's pantheon of unreliable narrators. Yet it is equally obvious that Ray—the principled opposite of Quilty's amoral decadence, who has been asked by Clarence Choate Clark, his cousin and Humbert's lawyer, to edit Humbert's manuscript—has a point. Just as Nabokov's postlude, "On a Book Entitled *Lolita*," frames the novel in aesthetic terms, so too does Ray's prelude frame it in ethical and even didactic terms. For him, *Lolita, or the Confession of a White Widowed Male* (with its arachnophobic connotations of a male black widow, the world's most poisonous spider) is nothing short of a cautionary tale and case history of child molestation. Humbert Humbert, "a shining example of moral leprosy," moves from thinking of Lolita as nothing more than an object that can be manipulated to fulfill his desire to thinking of her as a fully realized, fully rounded, hurt human being. Hence his is, in a very real sense, exactly as Ray claims, "a tragic tale tending unswervingly to nothing less than a moral apotheosis." (Humbert's killing of Quilty, as we shall see later on, is a far different matter.) All too menacingly true in our contemporary society, and perhaps even more timely now than when it first saw print in the seemingly composed and quiet 1950s, Humbert and Lo's story really does "warn us of dangerous trends" (5).

The point, then, is that *Lolita* is not an obscene book whose pornography, as Nabokov defines it in his afterword, "connotes mediocrity, commercialism, and certain strict rules of narration," and whose action "has to be limited to the copulation of clichés." *Lolita* is not a novel that consists of "an alternation of sexual scenes . . . the passages in between . . . reduced to sutures of sense, logical bridges of the simplest design, brief expositions and explanations, which the reader will probably skip" (313); rather, it is an ethical book about obscenity. It is not a book that transgresses moral boundaries, but a moral one about those boundaries and transgressions. While it is certainly true that we might at its outset discover patches of erotic prose lacing its pages, only a brash reader could misinterpret what he or she finds in them as "dirty." Nabokov's novel is an impassioned attack against human insensitivity, against our all-too-frequent inability to grant another human being freedom and individuality. And, from this perspective, it is nothing less than a deeply moving, deeply moral monograph important for Nabokov to have written, Olympia Press to have published, and us to have read.

LOLITA IN REEL TIME

An abbreviated look at the delightfully funny 1962 film version of *Lolita* will be illuminating at this point because director Stanley Kubrick's staid interpretation of Nabokov's book underscores the public's routine shortsightedness with regard to the novel's moral marrow. Gone from the 152-minute movie are the emotional extremes present in the prose. Gone is the psychological, geographical, and linguistic scope. The consequence is a steadier, safer, cleaner, smaller universe than the one Nabokov originally portrayed—and, it might well be argued, a more faded and flat one as well. A fine instance of the film's conservative impulse is what happens during Quilty's murder scene. In the novel Nabokov gives us Humbert's extended stalking and shooting of Quilty at Pavor Manor; Humbert devilishly wounds complaining Quilty repeatedly, eventually (and aptly) dogging him to the master bedroom, where Humbert the Horrible kills clearly guilty Quilty as the playwright, coughing and spitting up blood, ludicrously wraps himself in his bedclothes. In the film, though, after a quick couple of bullets on Humbert's part, most of which miss the mark, Quilty crawls off stage à la Greek tragedy to die behind a decorous eighteenth-century painting of an actress.

The film thus becomes as subtly suggestive as Lolita's gentle hip undulations as she hoola-hoops in the backyard, Humbert Humbert happily pretending to read nearby. Yet it also paradoxically becomes much more realistic in flavor, emphasizing as it does the first half of the novel and downplaying the hallucinatory and grotesque qualities that increasingly suffuse it. So while in the book Humbert's first other-worldly meeting with Quilty at the Enchanted Hunters hotel is couched in shadows and verbal static, in the motion picture the scene is portrayed as wacky but straightforwardly lifelike. And, save for some stock footage of a motel here and an aerial view of a town there, the important sense of roadside America is likewise downplayed (for good reason: the film was shot in England). Hence we find England's screenless windows, brick walls, and foggy countryside as Humbert drives toward Pavor Manor to execute Quilty; an English estate when he arrives; and, when Humbert visits Lolita and her husband Dick on (Enchanted?) Hunter Road in Coalmont, something looking a lot more like a British flat than the novel's very American "clapboard shack, with two or three similar ones farther away from the road and a waste of withered weeds all around" (269). The film furthermore downplays that which makes Nabokov's novel truly novel: the richness of its language, its dexterous tonal shifts, its deft, dense irony. While there do appear a few narrative overdubs, such as Humbert's description of his and Charlotte's wedding, by and large Nabokov's signature language slips into the background. So too does Humbert's point of view. We see him almost completely from the outside, and hence are denied the full ambivalent complexity of his character. What is said and done therefore dwarfs the greater importance of what remains unsaid and solely deviously thought.

Nabokov, as it happened, had little to say about all of this. Producer James B. Harris and director Stanley Kubrick acquired the film rights to *Lolita* in 1958. An American moviemaker living in England, Kubrick would come over the next decade to garner praise for such unhinged works as *Dr. Strangelove* (1963), *2001: A Space Odyssey* (1968), and the adaptation of *Lolita*'s kindred spirit, *A Clockwork Orange* (1971), Anthony Burgess's seemingly equally unfilmable linguistic extravaganza of a novel. In July 1959 Nabokov traveled from Europe to Hollywood to meet Harris and Kubrick about the possibility of doing the screenplay, but turned them down after being informed during early discussions that given the American censorial mind, it might be a savvy idea to create the impression by the movie's conclusion that Humbert and Lolita had actually been married all along. By 1960 Kubrick relented, however, promising the novelist more freedom. Nabokov returned to Hollywood and met with Harris and Kubrick at Universal City Studios on 1 March. The next morning, ensconced in a rented Californian villa, the author of *Lolita* began its screenplay, an act he felt was "rather like making a series of sketches for a painting that has long ago been finished and framed" (*SO*, 6). In June the first rendition was done: a nearly 400-page, unwieldy, tentative, digressive monster, which according to Kubrick would have taken nearly seven hours to run. Months of cutting and polishing ensued, but in September Kubrick finally gave the script his OK. Soon thereafter he commenced filming—without, however, involving Nabokov in the process. Unbeknown to the novelist at the time, Kubrick in his adaptation would end up using only about 20 percent of Nabokov's screenplay, which had, among other things, reinstated scenes dropped from early drafts of the book, transposed others, amplified dialogue, and inserted self-conscious visuals to highlight the idea of artifice in the film. On 13 June 1962 the movie premiered in New York to mainly positive reviews, but its box office success lasted only a few weeks. Not long after its popularity waned, Kubrick announced that the motion picture version of *Lolita* was his solitary major failure and claimed he probably wouldn't try to make it if he had it all to do over again. Nabokov was customarily much kinder in his appraisal. "I thought the movie was absolutely first-rate," he told Alvin Toffler in his 1964 *Playboy* interview. "The four main actors deserve the highest praise" (*SO*, 21). But he was also quick to add that "it is not what I wrote" (*SO*, 105), and that "people who liked my novel said the film was too reticent and incomplete" (*SO*, 49).

Several awkward choices concerning the movie were made by both director and writer. First off, it begins with the novel's finale: Quilty's slaying. In one of the film's most impressive scenes, Humbert Humbert plays a dark round of Ping-Pong with the playwright before snuffing him. Quilty magically produces little white ball after little white ball from his sleeve while Humbert Humbert magically produces his gun. Elated by how much he appears to be winning, inattentive Quilty has no idea to what an extent he's about to lose. The scene is therefore not only blackly, ironically, bizarrely funny in a quintessentially Nabokovian mode, but it also spotlights one of the principle leitmotifs running through both movie and novel: gaming. Granted the film's Ping-Pong has replaced the fiction's tennis as dominant sport, but it also puts us on the lookout for another game: that important chess match that takes place a couple of scenes on, when Charlotte (and not Gaston Godin, as in the novel) with good reason worries that Humbert Humbert is about to steal her queen. Because of the murder scene's placement, the remainder of the movie, set as much as four years earlier, becomes an extended flashback accounting for why Humbert kills Quilty. The effect of this, wed with the fact that we don't learn of Humbert Humbert's death by heart attack until the film's epilogue (and of Lolita's death not at all), is to water down the sense of murky McFatedness that rushes through the book. Also, setting the climactic murder scene at the alpha rather than the omega of the movie means that everything after it comes dangerously close to skidding into pallid celluloid afterthought.

An even more awkward choice was Nabokov's refusal to let a real child act Lolita's role. Sue Lyons, talented as she is, is clearly no nymphet. Rather, she appears on the silver screen as a full-fledged 17 going on 23. Humbert Humbert does once apply his favorite term to her, but its application rings hollow since we're never given his obsessively detailed definition. So Lyons comes off as wide-eyed, sensuous, and slinky, full-blossomed yet bratty. She can deliver a knockout goodnight kiss on Humbert's cheek, yet turn around and find Poe's poetry, which Humbert recites to her in his room, "corny." Kubrick, as it were, agrees with Nabokov's choice of an older Lolita by minimizing the erotic aspects of Humbert's relationship with her, hinting at them more through verbal puns than through physical gestures. While Humbert and Lo virtually don't kiss on the lips in the film, let alone touch one another intimately, the former can answer Charlotte's question about what made up his mind to rent a room from her by looking directly at Lolita sunning in the garden and saying: "Your cherry pies." And Lo, we discover, summers, not at the more understated Camp Q, as in the novel, but at Camp Climax. Nor does the potential for violence exist between Humbert and Lo as it does in the book. Hum never lays a hand on her in anger. He seldom raises his voice—certainly no more toward her than she toward him. And only one image from the film really alludes to the suffering Lo endures in the alternate space of the novel: the Gainsboroughesque painting of the young woman behind which Quilty dies. Humbert's riddling it with bullets suggests the abuse he inflicts on Lolita in his drive to "solipsize" her.

Interesting as well about that painting is the way the camera tightens on the young woman's eyes at the moment the shots pierce her face. This filmic decision flags another key leitmotif in the movie: the emphasis on seeing, on voyeurism, on radically subjective perception, and on Humbert's hope to turn Lo, Charlotte, and Quilty into the objects of his gaze, from his peeking at Lolita through the wall of flowers at the sedate school dance to the seemingly ubiquitous presence of eyeglasses in the movie. Indeed, those dark spectacles Lo wears when Humbert initially meets her seem to transmute in the course of the movie to the suggestion of Quilty's black-rimmed ones she wears when Humbert sees her for the last time (hardly, by the way, "hopelessly worn at seventeen" [277], as the novel has it), as if to say Lolita has in these few short years dropped her naïve perspective on the world and come to see and understand things from Quilty's decadent perspective.

If during her transubstantiation from fiction to film Lolita grows older, during his Humbert grows meeker. James Mason civilizes and tames his charming character so much that he almost completely fails to capture Humbert the Terrible's menacing side. No longer the sinister, obsessed pervert from the pages of Nabokov's novel, Hum here comes closer to an elegantly accented, love-smitten fool. He is obviously British, not the amalgam of all Europe as in the book, and now has a stable lectureship in French awaiting him in Ohio the autumn after he meets Lo—a suitable situation indeed, since this is a story about Humbert's *and* Lo's education. But it remains unclear how he made a living before journeying to the United States, mentions of his successful former scholarship notwithstanding. In fact, the whole of Humbert's past remains unclear, if not nonexistent, in the film. He has practically no history: no childhood, no Annabel, no series of breakdowns, only the merest insinuation of his first wife, Valeria.

Consequently, his perverse pedophilia commutes into airier love, or perhaps simply into a midlife crush on a young woman half (but surely no less) his age.

Mason solidifies this impression by making Humbert into a lovable bumbler who can't dance, can't even unfold his cot, while Bob Harris's romantically lush "Lolita Theme" and Nelson Riddle's syrupy soundtrack reinforce the schmaltzy feel of Humbert and Lo's relationship. As the opening credits roll, and the thick music sounds, and Humbert Humbert's hands caressingly apply polish to Lolita's toenails, any inkling of the corrupt and abusive evaporates. It actually seems out of place when, as Humbert, Lolita, and Charlotte sit sardined in their car at the drive-in, Peter Cushing's monstrous visage from *The Curse of Frankenstein* (1957) fills the screen, forming an obvious (if debatable) objective correlative for Humbert's desire. Here Humbert doesn't need to go through any moral apotheosis, doesn't need to realize what he's done is wrong, because he hasn't done much immoral or wrong with Lolita.

He remains in many ways little more than a jilted lover, gaining our sympathy especially through his relationship with shrill, crass, leopard-skin-dressed Charlotte Haze, who is played outstandingly by Shelley Winters. Even more brash in the film than in the fiction, Charlotte is chair of a great books club, boastful of the chain on her European flush toilet, proud of the cheap reproductions of predictable paintings by Dufy, Van Gogh, and Monet hanging on her walls, so much the essential American that her phone number is Ramsdale 1776. We begin to find ourselves deeply charitable toward Humbert in light of this.

The happiest surprise in the movie is Peter Sellers's marvelously off-kilter rendition of Quilty. A relatively minor player in the novel in terms of the scant number of pages devoted to him, Quilty nevertheless takes a prominent position in the film. A wonderfully nefarious, genuinely Nabokovian wackiness reveals itself in Sellers's proto-Strangelovean, thickly bespectacled rendition of Freudian Dr. Zemph, the kooky German pseudopsychologist from Beardsley High School who visits Humbert at home to con him into letting Lolita act in Quilty's play; his wild ramblings on the porch of the Enchanted Hunters hotel, where the word "normal" saturates a scene that is anything but; his dazzlingly protean accent that samples American dialects in a way the book doesn't; and his ominously chic dance number with the ever-silent and eerie Vivian Darkbloom. It should thus come as no jolt that Nabokov himself thought it an excellent idea in retrospect when a critic suggested that Sellers should have played Humbert Humbert instead of Quilty. Splendid as Sellers may have been for the part of Quilty, however, the film still diffuses the novel's impulse toward the terrestrially and cosmically sinister by quieting references to the playwright's blue movies, erasing the drug overtones associated with him, and downplaying the larger-than-life malevolence of McFatedness many readers think of when they think of Quilty.

If Sellers-as-Quilty at times lends the film something approaching an authentically Nabokovian mood, so too does the sportive sense of self-reflexivity imbuing it. Tongue in cheek, for example, the movie alludes to a good number of masterpieces from art history, thereby reminding us of the motion picture's own existence as a piece of calculated artifice crafted by a winking writer and wry moviemaker. We find ourselves suddenly viewing a parody of Jacques-Louis David's painting, *The Death of Marat,* depicting the political leader's murder by a young woman (named, significantly enough, *Charlotte* Corday) in his tub, when Humbert sloshes tipsily in his own tub shortly after Charlotte Haze's death, drink balancing on chest, gun nearby, bathroom slowly and comically filling with concerned friends and acquaintances. Humbert is by implication transmogrified into a martyr for the greater glory of love—although, of course, at the moment no one present except Humbert knows toward whom his revolutionary love is really channeled. Another martyr to love (or at least to Charlotte's schlocky take on it) is her deceased husband Harold, whose ashes we discover are farcically framed by a Byzantine triptych in her bedroom. Lo's seductive and scantily clad pose while sunning in the backyard during Humbert's and our first full sighting of her recalls the tradition of the reclining nude, especially such spicy and controversial renderings of it as Edouard Manet's *Olympia.*

Moreover, Kubrick tips his hat toward various classic movies and actors throughout his undertaking, just as Nabokov does toward various classic fictions throughout his. The first words Quilty speaks (wrapped in a toga-like sheet) announce him as Spartacus, a verbal nod to Kubrick's 1960 motion-picture epic by the same name. The sappily sentimental love scenes, such as the one in which Lo runs upstairs prior to starting out with her mother on her fateful ride to Camp Climax and passionately (nigh melodramatically) embraces Humbert, making him promise never to forget her, refer more generally to the great Hollywood romances of the 1930s and 1940s. And the slapstick scene in the Enchanted Hunters, in which the loud porter and poor Humbert flop and flail trying to unfold the cot while Lo sleeps peacefully nearby, lovingly looks back to Chaplin and Keaton, Laurel and Hardy, for its inspiration.

Emblematic of this admirable if understated film's self-reflexive urge is that in the original screenplay for it Vladimir Nabokov was going to play a butterfly hunter ("That nut with the net," Lo calls him[3]) named Vladimir Nabokov. Lost with Lolita on a dirt road in a canyon out west, Humbert was to ask him directions, thereby unconsciously paying homage not only to Alfred Hitchcock and the famous cameos he made in his movies but also, according to Nabokov, to Shakespeare, the bard himself (and one of Nabokov's major muses), who purportedly took on the role of the father's ghost in *Hamlet,* that extremely Nabokovian drama with revenge, possible (and possibly faked) insanity, self-reflexive plays within plays, the suggestion of sexual depravity, and murder at its heart.

HUMBERT THE HUMBLE, HUMBERT THE HOUND

Whereas Kubrick's motion picture presents us with a sophisticated, docile, and foolishly lovesick Humbert Humbert, Nabokov's novel presents us with a complex, paradoxical, and ultimately sinister if ultimately understandable one. His alias points to his intrinsic double nature. Invented, John Ray, Jr., informs us, by the author of *Lolita, or the Confession of a White Widowed Male* himself, this "bizarre cognomen" becomes a kind of "mask—through which two hypnotic eyes seem to glow" (3). It recalls "Monsieur Poe-Poe" (the French pun on "posterior" surely intentional), the name by which one of Humbert's Parisian students used to refer to "the poet-poet" (43), hence equating the twentieth-century prisoner composing his defense while awaiting trial for killing Clare Quilty with the nineteenth-century writer of ratiocinative tales that frequently focus on homicide, the presence of psychological twins, and radically unreliable narrators in states of emotional extremis. The name's "double rumble," Nabokov remarked, is "very nasty, very suggestive. It is a hateful name for a hateful person" (*SO*, 26). Alfred Appel, Jr., in his notes to *The Annotated Lolita*, perceptively comments that it is also one, if pronounced with the French accent from Humbert's childhood on the Riviera, that carries within it shadows of the Spanish words *ombre* ("shade") and *hombre* ("man"). This effectively offers Humbert as both the phantom-side of us all and a kind of midcentury Everyman—a scathing indictment on Nabokov's part about what it means to be human. That inherent stutter between Humbert's surname and given accordingly conjures questions concerning identity, psychological doubling, mirroring, subjective perception, and even memory itself, all of which are helpful thematic moorings to keep in mind while navigating Nabokov's text.

It is easy while under sail, however, to be swept up by that text's tidal tug into the powerful sway of those hypnotic eyes aglow behind that mask, easy to forget the "cesspoolful of rotting monsters" awrithe behind Humbert's "slow boyish smile" (44). After all, his language is gorgeous, his sense of humor mischievously splendid, his wide-ranging and whetted intelligence without reproach. Yet we should always be aware that no one can and no one should defend his behavior—in spite of the fact that he's intent on trying to defend it himself. A quick catalog of his crimes and misdemeanors makes the point. His protests and excuses to the contrary, Humbert is first and foremost a murderer. Worse, he is a murderer who can parenthetically comment (only a few weeks earlier having premeditatedly gunned down Quilty): "if I ever commit a *serious* murder . . . Mark the 'if'" (47, italics mine). By all means mark it, since its sense is that Quilty's murder isn't serious, that Humbert isn't remorseful about it. Mark, too, that the murder is only the darkest part of the portrait. Although caught and imprisoned for killing Quilty, Humbert is equally guilty of child abuse and molestation. He steals Lolita's anatomy, early life, and autonomy, first isolating her from other children and adults to such an extent and for such periods of time that she feels "she had absolutely nowhere else to go" (142) but to Humbert's bed, and then methodically chipping away at her will power until she "sobs in the night—every night, every night—the moment I feigned sleep" (176). Nabokov's novel thereby reworks and perverts the Pygmalion myth, casting Humbert Humbert as the woman-hating king of Cyprus who longs to shape Galatea-Lolita into his creation. Except that here Galatea-Lolita refuses complete capitulation, the couple never marries, and Pygmalion-Humbert only fully falls in love with his invention after the ivory from which she's been hewn devolves once more into human, all-too-human flesh in that shack on Hunter Road in Coalmont. Till then, Humbert's special name for her simply underscores the distance he intends to maintain between his solipsized idea of "Lolita" and the mundane reality of "Dolores Haze" on the dotted line.

There is still more, much more. Charlotte, so wildly unclever about so wildly many things, skirts near a portion of the truth when she accuses Humbert, whose lecherous diary she has just burgled and read, of being "a detestable, abominable, criminal fraud" (96). He is responsible for statutory rape and de facto incest, lewd and lascivious behavior, assault and battery. A kidnapper, he transports a minor across state lines. A child and spouse abuser, he slaps Lolita across the face on at least one occasion, often forces her to copulate with him (even when she's sick), threatens to send her to reform school and worse if she doesn't go along with his wishes, deprives her of a normal formal education for a full year. He brings his fists down hard on his wife Valeria's knees and knows that by twisting her weak wrist he can get pretty much anything he wants from her. Obsessed with destroying mature women in favor of his third-sex nymphets, he plans drowning Charlotte at Hourglass Lake and ponders strangling Miss Pratt at Beardsley School. He bribes his stepdaughter with money so she'll engage in sex with him, then steals the money back after the event. He repeatedly lies to the jury, to his psychiatrists, to Charlotte, to Lolita, to himself, and to a host of others. He bullies and blackmails. He side-swipes a stopped car without slowing down. He tears up a traffic ticket. Parked with Lo near schools to view the departing girl-children during the couple's 52-week cross-country odyssey that lasts from August 1947 to August 1948, he regularly takes on the role of voyeur. He is cruel in his meticulous attention to Lo's aging. He is excessive in his drinking, from those favorite "pins" (pineapple-juice-plus-gins) to a wide array of other spirits, and slowly unravels in the course of the novel into a state approaching alcoholism.

In these politically correct times, he is also guilty of effete elite snobbism. Nor do many narcissistic narrators in the history of literature go on with quite such zest about their good looks as Humbert le Bel, that "great big handsome hunk of movieland manhood" (39)—his big-boned body, exceedingly large hands, hairy chest, thick black eyebrows, strange accent, and later assertion that he's not "a glamour man" (283) notwithstanding. And, notwithstanding, his recurring references to himself as an ape, a wasp, a snake, a hound, and "a humble hunchback abusing myself in the dark" (62). No wonder his colors are often the obvious black and gray, and often the less so white-and-lilac of "those inflated spiders you see in old gardens" (49).

In spite of his old-world origins, Humbert embraces three of the four traits D. H. Lawrence claimed essential to the American soul. He is hard, he is isolate, and he is a killer.[4] But he has even more in common with the maverick artist associated with European romanticism, notably the Byronic version of it. Humbert is a solitary, gloomy, excessively self-conscious rebel on an unending quest for the unattainable. It thus comes as no surprise that the pages of his tale are abundant with allusions to Aeolian harps and a slew of English, French, and American romantic writers, including Keats, Blake, Byron, Rousseau, and (by far most often cited) Poe; rife with mentions of Humbert's "infinite melancholy" (17), his "romantic soul" (53), his medically and metaphorically unhealthy heart, and the "hot, opalescent, thick tears that poets and lovers shed" (52); rich in emphasis on his role as social outcast, a martyr to the absolute, the Satanic hero-villain, and the glorious outlaw; and strewn with references to the "miserably unattainable" (239) and "the great promised—the great rosegray never-to-be-had" (264). He is obsessed with his pursuit of the elusive and destructive Lolita in the same way Melville's Ahab is obsessed with his pursuit of the elusive and destructive Moby-Dick. His ruinous education into the gulf between the ideal and the real looks back to dreamy Emma Bovary's in Flaubert's nineteenth-century novel. And, like Conrad's Kurtz, Humbert is a tortured romantic exploring the heart of darkness in a deromanticized era. In the afterword, Nabokov fittingly and snidely dubs his protagonist an "anarchist" (315), and it is meticulously suitable that this amoral nonconformist intent on disregarding social conventions remains unclear about his legal status with Lolita throughout his affair with her.

Another link that unites him with romantic artists is his perception of time. For Humbert, two modes of it exist. One is *chronos,* communal time that registers chronology, mathematical sequence, a change of state, scientific cause and effect. This is the time of prosaism, details, inevitable death, the world of realism. Opposed to this is *kairos,* or divine time, an intensely subjective time that stands outside cause and effect. This is the time of poetry, love, immortality, the fantastic interval of romance, fairy tales, legends, myths, surrealism, and so on.[5] Humbert keenly feels the pain of *chronos* and longs through art to attain the transcendental realm of *kairos.* Put simply, his purpose is to create a supreme fiction entitled *Lolita, or the Confession of a White Widowed Male* to shore the fragments of his and Lo's lives against the supreme facts: time and its rhythmic lover, death. Living in Europe, Nabokov himself avidly read Henri Bergson and clearly took away with him the French philosopher's emphasis on subjective time and his rejection of scientific time, but Humbert's notions on the matter come closer to Poe's in "The Poetic Principle." The romantic poet's infatuation with the absolute of perfect beauty, Poe writes, is like the unquenchable "desire of the moth for the star . . . It is no mere appreciation of the Beauty before us—but a wild effort to reach the Beauty above. Inspired by an ecstatic prescience of the glories beyond the grave, we struggle, by multiform combinations among the things and thoughts of Time, to attain a portion of that Loveliness whose very elements, perhaps, appertain to eternity alone."[6] The act of writing becomes for Humbert a quest after "that intangible island of entranced time" (17), that "refuge of art" (309), where Lolita, whom he views as his vehicle to the divine, will never grow up, the poison of mortality never enter her veins. Humbert yearns to freeze his young lover in a glistening moment of flawless Keatsian stasis as she stretches her legs across his lap that magical Sunday morning, or whacks at the white ball on that sunny tennis court, because he understands only too well that, just as Shakespeare repeatedly understood in his sonnets, "this is the only immortality you and I may share" (309). It is fitting, then, that the name Hourglass Lake drifts through the pages of the book's first half, since ailing Humbert is keenly aware that, as he composes his narrative, time is literally running out for him.

Unlike the romantics, though, Humbert's goal is seldom truth with a capital T. Possibly the most insidious aspect of his personality is his ability to sound convincing while lying through his teeth. Early in his confession he confidently claims to have a photographic memory (40). If we take him at his word on this matter (always an iffy proposition on our part), then we must surmise that when he flubs a fact he's deliberately falsifying. But the line between truth and trick is fuzzy at best in umber and black Humberland, especially when 177 pages on he reverses his claim by asserting that his memory is really "incomplete" (217). Notice how he typically slides from fact to fancy in the following two sentences: "The stipulation of the Roman law, according to which a girl may marry at twelve, was adopted by the Church, and is still preserved, rather tacitly, in some of the United States. And fifteen is lawful everywhere" (135). The assertion about the Roman law is accurate enough, although much more intricate than Humbert would have us believe, as is the one about its adoption by the Church. But "some of the United States" actually means only 10 (Colorado, Florida, Idaho, Kansas, Louisiana, Maine, Maryland, Massachusetts, Tennessee, Virginia), and "lawful everywhere" is wholly erroneous, since the age in 17 states (Alaska, Arizona, California, Connecticut, Delaware, Illinois, Indiana, Michigan, Minnesota, Montana, Nebraska, Nevada, New Mexico, Ohio, Pennsylvania, West Virginia, and Wyoming) is 16, and in 2 (New Hampshire and New Jersey) 18.

This rhetorical strategy of playing fast and loose with accuracy is omnipresent in Humbert's story. Another notable instance occurs when he defends his affair with a minor by claiming that it belongs to a long (and therefore somehow acceptable) tradition of history's great literary lovers like Poe and Virginia Clemm, Dante and Beatrice, and Petrarch and Laura. True: Poe was 27 when he married his nymphetic 13-year-old cousin. Humbert, however, adroitly forgets to mention that Dante was only 9 when he first met 8-year-old Beatrice in 1274 and that there is no evidence to suggest that Laura was substantially younger than 23-year-old Petrarch when they met in 1327. And, it goes without saying, the assertion that what Humbert has with Lolita is a love affair is at best a highly debatable point. Is theirs really a romance? Can a tale about an unhinged man's nympholepsy and methodical ability to rob a young girl of her independence, individuality, and youth sincerely be about love? The answer is yes—but only if viewed from the exceptionally subjective perspective of a remarkably unsound, socially marginalized mind.

We need to be ceaselessly on our guard against Humbert's elocutionary guile. An even more overt illustration of his flair for falsification is the scene in which he plots Charlotte's demise. At the instant he's about to shove her beneath the waters of Hourglass Lake and hold her there while shouting for help from the two men on the opposite bank, he claims his resolve dissolves: "But what d'ye know, folks—I just could not make myself do it!" (87; note in passing the playful diction that undercuts Humbert's sincerity). Why can't he go through with it? One, because Charlotte's ghost would haunt him *Hamlet*-style for the rest of his days. And, two, because "the majority of sex offenders . . . are innocuous, inadequate, passive, timid strangers who merely ask the community to allow them to pursue their practically harmless, so-called aberrant behavior, their little hot wet private acts of sexual deviation without the police and society crackling down upon them. We are not sex fiends! We do not rape as good soldiers do. We are unhappy, mild, dog-eyed gentlemen. . . . Emphatically, no killers are we. Poets never kill" (87–88).

Sex offenders, he avows, aren't really mean-souled abusers and obsessed molesters. Rather, they're "innocuous," "inadequate," "passive," "timid," "practically harmless." Their behavior isn't dangerous, only so-called aberrant by a community obviously ignorant of the ramifications of cultural relativism. Such offenders ("We are not sex fiends!") thus become less violators of social codes than victims of them in a repressive society whose police "crackl[e] down" on the morally inoffensive. They don't rape "as good soldiers do" (notice two things here: first, that Humbert again fudges, since in truth he's blameworthy of statutory rape, putting himself in league with those "good" soldiers; and, second, that he tries to imply his innocence by insinuating those "good" soldiers' guilt, thereby suggesting that two grotesque wrongs equal one bright right). No longer a handsome hunk of movieland manhood in this passage, Humbert suddenly shape-shifts for purposes of his defense and our mercy into an "unhappy, mild, dog-eyed gentleman." Apparently overlooking that "you can always count on a murderer for a fancy prose style" (9), he now asserts that "poets never kill." Careful readers know differently. His miraculously controlled language gives the lie to his earlier allegation that he has no freewill, that he's merely "a plaything" of "that devil of mine" (56). He's sly. He's circumspect. He's ominously autonomous, even as he attempts to elicit our sympathy.

Nabokov emphasizes his own condemnation of Humbert in a delectably, subtly Nabokovian way. At Camp Q to retrieve Lolita on the heels of Charlotte's death, Humbert watches the camp mistress write him a receipt. As he does so he predictably takes note of the photos of girls placed here and there, but also of the sounds of birds in the background, a framed diploma, and, significantly, "some gaudy moth or butterfly, still alive, safely pinned to the wall" (110). Later, during the southern course of the couple's first 27,000-mile cross-country trek, he remarks in passing on some yucca blossoms, "so pure, so waxy, but lousy with creeping white flies" (156). And, later still, near the start of the midwestern stretch of their journey, halted briefly at a gas station where Lo surreptitiously conveys information to Quilty, Humbert fleetingly comments on his environment: a green garbage can, whitewalled tires for sale, a red icebox, and "that bug patiently walking up the inside of the window of the office" (211). In each case, Nabokov has Humbert err in his entomology. In the first instance he can't tell the flagrant difference between a moth and a butterfly (though the diligent reader should fathom at once the analogy between beautiful Lolita and the insect, both snared, both pinned alive to the wall by their hunters). In the second, he confuses female Yucca Moths with common flies. And, in the third, he fails to take the time to differentiate among a moth, a fly, and a beetle, eliding all three possibilities together into that ambiguous bug on the inside of the office window. A cutting inculpation by the master entomologist himself, the drift of these passages is that Humbert is blind to whole solar systems swirling within his cosmos—an accusation borne out by the leitmotif of sunglasses that runs through the book and suggests partial vision, dark sightedness, and solipsistic perception.

Humbert is hence an unreliable narrator par excellence, joining the American literary tradition that includes such fallible first-person storytellers as Mark Twain's Huck Finn and Henry James's governess in *The Turn of the Screw*. Humbert's comprehension, interpretation, and evaluation of his situation and the situation of others are regularly radically opposed to the implicit ones of the author. If there were ever any question about the matter, Nabokov stresses Humbert's unbalanced psychology by accentuating not only his connections with Poe's gallery of untrustworthy raconteurs but also Humbert's multiple stays in sanatoriums for bouts of insanity—if, Humbert is quick to add, "to melancholia and a sense of insufferable oppression that cruel term must be applied" (34). And plainly it must. All the events recounted in his confession are filtered through one man's warped consciousness. Humbert carefully manipulates his discourse, over which he is monarch, Humbert the Hummer, selecting, interpreting, and altering details for his own ends. His first-person point of view tends to win our sympathy, primarily during our early readings of the text, because its mouthpiece is savvy, cultivated, fairly well-off, wonderfully educated, and witty. As Nomi Tamir-Ghez indicates, Humbert both appeals to the jury's reason ("Gentlewomen of the jury! Bear with me! Allow me to take just a tiny bit of your precious time!" [123]) and pokes fun at it ("Frigid gentlewomen of the jury!" [132]) with the intent to ingratiate himself with the reader, who, he implies, is not as conventional in his or her way of thinking as the socially sanctioned court. Moreover, he plays it double-safe by making sure Lolita is seldom quoted, thus virtually erasing her point of view from the pages of his book all together.

True: at close range much of what Humbert says makes good sense. In his "tangle of thorns" (9), he comes to seem a penitent over time, a confessor, a martyr to a divine kind of love. At the same time it is just the width between his use of such a sacred Christian symbol as that crown of thorns and the golden tongue he shares with Milton's Satan that we should keep in mind. We must repeatedly draw back and evaluate critically his opinions and observations about himself and his world—a world, we should always understand, which proves to be a terribly hermetic one. Just *how* terribly hermetic might be gleaned by imagining Humbert's tale retold from a third-person point of view. What effect would such a change in narrative perspective have on the reader? To begin, an immense fissure would yawn between Humbert and ourselves. Divorced from his consciousness, we would suddenly see him mainly from the outside, through his actions, rather than mainly from the inside, through his thoughts and feelings, and we would thus find it much easier to judge him: the space between public fact and private fantasy would become dizzyingly apparent, its forbidding flavor flagged. Accordingly, Humbert would turn into nothing but that detestable, abominable, criminal fraud Charlotte saw in him.

But things are never quite so facile in Nabokov's universe. We should be just as wary of Charlotte's limited point of view as we are of Humbert's. Granted: Humbert is perverted, unreliable, mentally unstable. Even "evil" may not be too strong a word for him. He is plainly guilty of all the charges we have so far leveled against him, and probably others betimes. Nevertheless, he is more than that as well. Because we hear his story conveyed through his voice, we come to see that at times he is also sadly sympathetic, at times hurtfully human, almost always (if nothing else) spookily understandable. *Lolita* is therefore not so much a novel about Humbert Humbert's being on trial before a jury (with each reader as final judge) as it is a book about his being on trial before himself, a trial during which he finds himself painfully lacking. From this angle, the narrative is finally one of education—not only Lo's and ours concerning the horrors inherent in humanity but also Hum's concerning the horrors inherent in himself. No doubt he spiderishly spins a host of half-truths and flat-out lies. No doubt his devious rhetorical control is amazing. Nonetheless, he is also regularly agonizingly honest about the beast within, and honest in a way that makes him both extremely humorous and extremely human. He learns at last on his quest of self-accusation and self-justification that he possesses two of the most severe limitations on human consciousness that Nabokov believes one can. First, Humbert is stuck in the prisonhouse of the self, unable to transcend his own mind and enter those of others; hence, *Lolita* indeed becomes a kind of love story, a narrative about one person's near inability to achieve humane love with another. Second, Humbert is stuck in the prisonhouse of the present, unable to reach his own magical past, bound on all sides by *chronos,* which he longs to surpass by means of memory and imagination; not for nothing, then, does he find himself a dying man in a jail cell composing a confession of his sins and his love, while Nabokov in his afterword relates the haunting seed-story for *Lolita* about the ape in the Jardin des Plantes, whose first drawing was a sketch of nothing less than the bars on its own cage (311). The correspondence between Humbert and ape is conspicuous. Brigs abound in this book.

Furthermore, just because we can't believe everything Humbert Humbert asserts doesn't mean we can't believe anything he asserts. Listening to that golden tongue of his soon leads us into the country of Epimenides's paradox, which asks us to consider the following phrase: "This sentence is not true." Now: is the sentence true, or not? If it is true, then it isn't; if it's not, then it is. If a liar such as Humbert shows us that he sometimes lies, is it equally true that he sometimes tells the truth? How do we know? Some readers have made the case that it's impossible to do so, that we can't really trust anything Humbert says.[7] He claims, for instance, that he didn't deflower Lolita, that the guilty party was Charlie Holmes at Camp Q. He claims, too, that he didn't seduce Lolita that morning at the Enchanted Hunters, that it was Lolita who seduced him. Do we believe him, knowing he has lied before? Some readers have argued the answer is no, clearly we can't and clearly we mustn't. These cases, they say, represent no more than further confabulations on Humbert's part. But others have argued the opposite. The solution? Surely in the end it all comes down to textual tone and readerly orientation. We will each hear Humbert's voice differently, emphasizing this passage, deemphasizing that. Some will discover a Humbert the Hound, others a Humbert the Humble, and still others both at once. Who we are will determine how we will hear Humbert's confession, how much credence we will give it, how we will piece together its puzzle.

Look, by way of illustration, at how Humbert accounts for his fixation on Lolita. He tells us he was born in 1910, raised in a posh hotel on the Riviera by his racially mixed father and English mother. At 13 he meets Annabel Leigh, a beautiful girl a few months his junior, also of mixed parentage, with whom he falls in love. Because of two botched trysts, the first interrupted by Annabel's mother calling her in from their villa garden for the evening, the second by two mysterious bathers abruptly emerging from the sea just as Humbert prepares to make love to Annabel on a secluded beach, the children are never able to consummate their relationship. Annabel dies of typhus on Corfu four months later. During his college days in London and Paris (he interestingly first planned to become a psychiatrist), Humbert begins searching out young-looking prostitutes and then, in an attempt to create the appearance of normalcy, he marries Valeria, daughter of a Polish doctor. Her sole appeal in Humbert's eyes is the fine imitation she does of a little girl. In 1939 an American uncle wills Humbert several thousand dollars on the condition he move to the United States and enter his uncle's perfume business writing ads. Before Valeria and Humbert can embark, however, he discovers she is having an affair with the taxi-driving colonel named Maximovich. Humbert and Valeria divorce. Now in his thirties, and now alone in New York at the outset of World War II, he suffers a mental breakdown, travels on an expedition to arctic Canada as part of the cure, and returns home— only to tumble into a second psychological collapse. Upon his release from a sanatorium in 1947, he decides to move to New England and spend a simple summer working on his comparative history of French literature for English-speaking students. He meets Lolita instead.

His blocked desire with Annabel, Humbert would have us believe, leads to his fixation on certain girls aged 9 to 14. His existence is thus predicated on his pursuit of the long-past affair, and the irony in this is that the illusion he pursues is real enough to undo him. Now: can we trust his tale? At first glance, certainly. Humbert has comfortably framed the picture of his life story within a Freudian paradigm, revealing that childhood traumas not only shape who we are but also dog us throughout our later years. Yet what are we then to make of the fact that Humbert's confession (the confession of someone who originally intended to take a degree in psychiatry) is riddled with anti-Freudian innuendo after anti-Freudian innuendo? Psychiatrists in the world according to Humbert Humbert are "dream-extortionists" (34), "tainted by the scholastic rigmarole and standardized symbols of the psychoanalytic racket" (285), with whom he sports at sanatoriums, teasing the hapless masters of the "libididream" (54) with made-up primal scenes and hints of his own homosexuality, even staying on an extra month just to delight in giving them a hard time. Mentions of the "shams and shamans" (259) who follow that "Viennese medicine man" (274) are sandwiched between mentions of soap operas and cheap novelettes (80), rapists (113), and fakes (124).

In addition, Humbert flaunts his knowledge of their business to lampoon its severely limited and deadeningly limiting systematic view of the human psyche. "We must remember," he bemusedly reminds us when describing the gun with which he will kill Quilty, "that a pistol is the Freudian symbol of the Ur-father's central forelimb" (216)—as if, he suggests, that might in some other universe be an intellectually interesting or psychologically insightful observation to make.

A psychiatrist interested in his case, Herr Doktor Humbert offers, might assume that Humbert the Terrible would take Lolita to the beach to seek psychic release from his frustrated encounter with Annabel. But no. He returns to the seaside with his nymphet for only "a purely theoretical thrill." Nor does anything change with respect to his nympholepsy because of this seaside visit (he remains, he admits, a nympholept to the end of his life [257]): "So much for those special sensations, influenced, if not actually brought about, by the tenets of modern psychiatry" (167).

Uncomfortable with the sting of his satiric venom, we might here try to argue that Humbert is venting anger against an earlier failed version of himself. Or we might search for evidence of the ironic distance between Humbert's and Nabokov's attitudes to further underscore the former's unreliability. We would come up empty handed on both accounts. Humbert only mentions his foray into psychiatry once (15), setting little store in it, and this time narrator and author are in perfect agreement. Known for what in his afterword he calls "my old feud with Freudian voodooism" (314), Nabokov in his interviews and fiction (especially *Lolita* and *Pale Fire*) repeatedly attacked the father of psychoanalysis and his followers for what he saw as their simplistic and restrictive generalizations about the workings of the human mind. "Let the credulous and the vulgar continue to believe that all mental woes can be cured by a daily application of old Greek myths to their private parts," he once told a critic. "I really do not care" (*SO,* 66).

We can hence hear Nabokov speaking to us through Humbert when Humbert naughtily inverts and thereby subverts Freud on creativity by saying that "it is not the artistic aptitudes that are secondary sexual characters . . . ; it is the other way around: sex is but the ancilla of art" (259). Art, to phrase it slightly differently, is not the Freudian sublimation of sexual desire and dysfunction, with the concomitantly dark and despotic vision of the creative process such a belief embraces. Rather, sexuality in Humbert's (and Nabokov's) dimension is the by-product of a richly and freely aesthetic outlook. Sexuality ("the oddly prepubescent curve of her back, her ricey skin, her slow languorous columbine kisses" [259]) is one manifestation among many of a generous perspective provided by the artistic temperament, be that temperament evinced by nature or narrator.

Can we then sometimes believe Humbert? Yes, but in an intricate and cautious way. We must always be alert, always listen to the tenor of his tone and check it against the hard evidence of the text. If we are and if we do, we shall hear toward the end of his manuscript that with increasing frequency he begins to drop the arch irony charging his diabolical rhetoric and become progressively more sincere. While oscillations between the sardonic and the straightforward, the facts and the falsifications, fluctuate till the last paragraph of the book, they do so with incrementally less commonness. Humbert briefly gives up his mocking style as early as chapter 25 in part 1, as he recalls his drive to

Camp Q to pick up Lo after Charlotte's death. There he announces, "Oh, let me be mawkish for the nonce! I am so tired of being cynical" and, six lines later, "Don't think I can go on. Heart, head—everything. Lolita, Lolita, Lolita, Lolita, Lolita, Lolita, Lolita, Lolita, Lolita. Repeat till page is full, printer" (109). Surely this is not Humbert the Hummer speaking. These sentences are indicative of another room in the confessor's consciousness. They reveal a real, hurt heart beneath a wry exterior.

Increasingly clear is that Humbert gradually comes to understand what he has done to Lolita, to know it is wrong, and to feel genuine remorse for it. As he recounts how he descended to the lobby in the Enchanted Hunters to wait for those sleeping pills to work on poor Dolly (his pet name for Lolita), Humbert-in-prison interrupts the narrative of Humbert-in-hotel to say his only regret is that he didn't turn in his room key at the office at that precise moment and abandon "the town, the country, the continent, the hemisphere,—indeed, the globe—that very same night" (123). As Dolly climbs into his car the next day, obviously in pain after her repeated copulations with him, Humbert comprehends that "this was a lone child, an absolute waif, with whom a heavy-limbed, foul-smelling adult had had strenuous intercourse three times that very morning. Whether or not the realization of a lifelong dream had surpassed all expectation, it had, in a sense, overshot its mark—and plunged into a nightmare" (140). It soon dawns on him that he is "only a brute" (193), "a pentapod monster" (284), and Lolita a "poor, bruised child" (284)—a discovery that leads him to hope that his "heart may rot" (a wish that quite literally comes true [205]).

During the last 30 pages of his manuscript Humbert speaks most forcefully about what John Ray, Jr., in his foreword calls Humbert's moral apotheosis. He does so first when he finds the bedraggled pregnant Dolly Schiller in her shoddy Coalmont shack; second as he prepares to take revenge on Quilty for stealing the symbol of Humbert's happiness from him; and third as he waits in his car on a grassy slope for the police to catch up shortly after the dirty deed. Humbert is shocked by the state in which he discovers Dolly, with her "ruined looks and her adult, rope-veined narrow hands and her gooseflesh white arms." So far so Humbert, from his apparently cruel focus on her infection by time to his disappointment that his object of desire has outgrown her nymphetdom and hence, we might expect, her usefulness. But what follows is surprising. As he stares at her sitting across from him, her simple and faithful husband puttering nearby on a neighbor's house, he learns something about himself, and we learn something about him: "[I] knew as clearly as I know I am to die," he says, "that I loved her more than anything I had ever seen or imagined on earth, or hoped for anywhere else. . . . You may jeer at me, and threaten to clear the court, but until I am gagged and half-throttled, I will shout my poor truth, I insist the world know how much I loved my Lolita, *this* Lolita, pale and polluted, and big with another's child" (277–78). Not only does Humbert cancel and curse his earlier relationship with Lolita, baptizing it as no more than sterile and selfish vice, but he also rejects the notion of "nymphet," which up to this point has been his raison d'être.

In passionate, stunning, and painfully candid prose, he accepts *this* Lolita, Dolly Schiller herself, with all her human frailty, and he renounces the one that was little more than a figment of his fancy. He finds her even more extraordinary now than then, complexly textured and fully alive, because she is free from his brutal solipsism. When he asks her to run away with him, she answers that she would sooner go back to Quilty, and hurt Humbert understands the burning gist of her statement. "*He* broke my heart," he knows she means. "*You* merely broke my life" (279). Although she ultimately refuses him, ending once and for all his ambition to possess a transcendental kingdom by the sea, he turns over the money that is rightfully hers without hesitation (another surprise for us if we remember that only two years and a little time ago he made a habit of stealing his bribes back from her), and withdraws after one more panged plea: "are you quite, quite sure that—well, some day, any day, you will not come to live with me? I will create a brand new God and thank him with piercing cries if you give me that microscopic hope" (280).

She turns him down. Devastated, he again becomes an enchanted hunter. This time Quilty, not Lolita, is his victim. In the midst of describing his deadly journey to Pavor Manor, Humbert once more breaks off his present-time narration to recollect two upsetting and revealing images of Lolita that bubble up from their earlier life together. The first is Lo turning to her friend Eva Rosen at twilight on a street in Beardsley (Humbert is escorting both to a concert) and out of the blue bluely remarking: "You know, what's so dreadful about dying is that you are completely on your own" (284). As the sun perishes, and Lo abruptly names death (which the reader knows will hook her on Christmas Day 1952), Humbert is dumbstruck. He recalls how uncomfortable they both waxed when trying to discuss abstract ideas that a daughter and parent or friend and friend might discuss, and he comes to see just how little he really knows about the Dolly beneath the Lolita, about what she thinks, feels, enjoys, fears. The second upsetting and revealing image is Lolita's fading smile as she watches her ornithoid friend Avis Byrd happily hug her father, her father lovingly return the hug. Replaying the scene in his mind's eye, Humbert is hit by the galactic abyss between Avis and her father's life, on the one hand, and his and Lolita's, on the other. And something else as well: "there were times when I know how you felt," he admits to himself and to us, "and it was hell to know it" (284–85).

In an act of purgation, he kills Quilty. The police overtake him as he drives from Parkington on the wrong side of the highway. In an attempt to avoid a roadblock, Humbert veers up a grassy slope into a pasture where he bumps to a stop. Waiting patiently for the law to reach him, he recalls another episode from his past. Shortly after Lo had left him for Quilty, he found himself existentially nauseated on a mountain road overlooking a mining town. From the amalgam of roofs and streets below, a miraculous sound wafted up to him, which he soon identified as "the melody of children at play." He stood listening to the funning and laughter, the smack of a baseball bat and the rattle of a toy wagon, and a thought troubled his spirit: "I knew that the hopelessly poignant thing was not Lolita's absence from my side, but the absence of her voice from that concord" (308).

Humbert's perception of Lolita metamorphoses through his narrative. His education into the human condition can be measured by the span of space between his initial conception of Lolita—as a sexual object created by his imagination to quench his unquenchable desire—and his final conception of Dolly Schiller—as an intellectually and emotionally resonant person imbued with free will. The trajectory of that education might well be enhanced by the presence of a fairly minor character in the work's web of events: Rita, the drunken divorcée Humbert picks up at a bar between Toylestown and Blake shortly after losing Lo. Exactly twice as old and occupying the same amount of time in Humbert's life as Lolita, Rita is the only exception to the general rule that Humbert hungers to destroy mature women (remember Valeria, Charlotte, Miss Pratt) in favor of his third-sex nymphets. She is "so kind" (258), "the sweetest, simplest, gentlest, dumbest Rita imaginable" (259). Despite that last all-too-charcteristic Humbertian adjective, and despite himself, Rita shows Humbert the Small something akin to mature camaraderie and possibly even whole-hearted compassion. She also sets him on a path away from invented nymphets and toward irrefutable humanity, allowing him to surpass his obsessive narcissism and grasp the horror of what he has done to Lolita, whom he finally learns to love honestly and plainly. It is this ultimate circuit Humbert's education takes that wins over many readers.

But just as we are ready to compliment this Dostoevskian underground man, this marginalized paradox of emotions and motivations, whom we have seen traverse both crime and punishment (those negative things Nabokov had to say about the nineteenth-century Russian writer notwithstanding), we come up short. After all, if it is true that Humbert has undergone a moral apotheosis by the end of his life and book, how could he have been able to recount with such perverse precision his earlier delights with Lolita? Is this just a narrative necessity on Nabokov's part, since without those unpleasant emotional and physical descriptions we would be unable to adequately understand the moral ground Humbert has covered? Or is it a portion of the process of Humbert's purgatory, needing as he does to confront the beast to pass beyond it? Or, as some have argued, is it simply another subtle Nabokovian revelation and accusation about his character's unreliability and unrepentant way of being in the world? Probably the first and the second combined, given the way novels need to work, but always possibly the third. If criticism on the subject is any clue, the answer once again will rest somewhere in the pages of the reader's own spiritual autobiography.

Of yet more import is that the surely unreliable John Ray, Jr., in his assertion that Humbert undergoes a moral apotheosis through his relationship with Lolita, obviously overlooks the flagrant fact that Humbert undergoes none whatsoever through his relationship with Clare Quilty, whom, after all, he unrepentantly murders in his memoir's momentous conclusion. In the narrative's penultimate paragraph Humbert levies his own verdict on himself: "Had I come before myself I would have given Humbert at least thirty-five years for rape, and dismissed the rest of the charges" (308). Nor should we pity Quilty, Humbert adds in the narrative's penultimate sentence, because "one had to choose between him and H. H., and one wanted him to make you [Lolita] live in the minds of later generations" (309). Surely this must be counted as huge hard evidence that Humbert has actually learned nothing about humanity, free will, and the evils of savage solipsism. Unless, that is, we read Quilty's character and murder metaphorically, remembering that, for all his earlier talk of killing, Humbert discovers he simply can't kill a soul except the one person who stole his hope for transcendent perfection. If we see Clare Quilty as Humbert's dark double (and a host of critics have), then his death becomes less (if at all) the literal liquidation of a person than it does the figurative erasure of Humbert's negative side. From this Jungian point of view, Quilty's homicide even adds credence to the allegation that Humbert weathers a sea change during the course of his education and finally, hero-like, plunges into the depths of his own psyche to do battle with his umber self, then resurfaces a more nearly integrated, if ultimately doomed, human being.

PAWN, QUEEN, MY POOR LITTLE GIRL

Still, all said and done, Nabokov disagreed with such positive readings of his protagonist. "Humbert Humbert is a vain and cruel wretch who manages to appear 'touching,'" he commented acerbically in a

The Moral Dimension: Umber and Black Humberland

Paris Review interview published in 1967. "That epithet, in its true, tear-iridized sense, can only apply to my poor little girl" (*SO*, 94). Here we are well-advised to remember that after a novel's publication its author becomes only one among a myriad of its acute critics, his opinion of that book's form, content, and motives no more or less valuable than that of any other perceptive reader, that we must learn to trust the tale and not necessarily the teller. Yet Nabokov's statement is worth contemplation, presenting us as it does with an instructive caveat. Exploring Lolita's character, it warns, we should remind ourselves that we view her solely through Humbert's warped if wistful consciousness, and that his aim is to lure us into being his vicarious partner in rape and murder and more. Since Humbert's narrative is told from the first-person point of view, as we have seen, we are never allowed to view Lolita (or, for that matter, any of the other characters or events in Humbert's confession) objectively. We seldom actually even hear her own words, and, when we do, we can't be completely sure if they really *are* her own words or if they have simply been put in her mouth by puppeteer Humbert to serve his dubious purposes. Emblematic of the ease with which we can slide into the enemy's camp is that many readers by the novel's conclusion have forgotten that the target of Humbert's desire is not in fact named "Lolita" at all, but "Dolores" or "Dolly Haze." Humbert's manipulation of our memory and her name points to how dexterously he is able to nudge us into the jagged terrain of his unsound psyche.

Searching for what to call his "poor little girl," Nabokov said he "needed a diminutive with a lyrical lilt. One of the most limpid and luminous letters is 'L.' The suffix '-ita' has a lot of Latin tenderness, and this I required too. Hence: Lolita." He went on to stress that the first syllable should be pronounced delicately, with a caress, as in the first syllable of the word "lollipop," Spanish- or Italian-style. But beneath the liquid beauty of "Lolita" stirs the hard heartache inherent in "Dolores Haze." Her given name derives from the Latin "dolor," literally meaning "sorrow" and "pain," and connotatively carrying with it the hint of "roses and tears," as Nabokov explained, because of its traditional associations with the Virgin Mary and the Seven Sorrows concerning the life of Jesus. As if to drive home the point, Humbert once describes Dolly as "crucified" against a door as he edges past her into her house on Hunter Road (270). Her surname derives from the German word for "hare," an appropriately defenseless if fecund prey to be hunted and haunted by Humbert's predatory lusts (*SO*, 25).

We meet her as her mother ushers recently arrived Humbert onto "the piazza" of her Ramsdale house one lush green day in late May 1947, and we are instantly made aware of the ironic chasm that gapes between Humbert's romantic ideal and the universe's prosaic real. Heady Humbert sees "from a mat in a pool of sun, half-naked, kneeling, turning about on her knees, . . . my Riviera love peering at me over dark glasses" (39), but the attentive reader sees only a cute, all-American, nose-picking, bubblegum-snapping, movie-magazine-reading, bike-riding, tanned, tomboyish seventh-grader with pale gray eyes, bright brown hair (not the blond of the movie version), a pretty plump lower lip, and a freckly snub-nose. Dolly was engendered on the Haze honeymoon in Vera Cruz, born 1 January 1935, raised in a midwestern town called Pisky (with its magical pun on "pixie"), and, after her father's death, brought to Ramsdale in New England in 1945 to live with her mother in the house of her late paternal grandmother. She is a typical 12-year-old who inhabits the mystifying Mason-Dixon line between bright preteen kid and naïve would-be adult. She is simultaneously coarse and witty, gullible and frank, physical and fragile.

But to Humbert, claiming special capacities of perception, she is a "nymphet," that particular portion of the female population between the ages of 9 and 14 that "is not human, but nymphic (that is, demoniac)" (16), possessing the power to bewitch older men by means of its devilish "twofold nature": "tender dreamy childishness" combined with "a kind of eerie vulgarity" (44). She thus descends from the Greek and Roman mythological nymphs, the alluring minor nature goddesses who lived in the sea like the Nereids, the forests like the Dryads, and the mountains like the Oreads (the chaste nymphs of Diana, we should note in passing, were often hounded by lecherous Humbertian satyrs). She also shares much metaphorically with the entomological nymph, a word in this context referring to the pupal stage of an insect undergoing incomplete metamorphosis, as well as to the various nymphalid butterflies often characterized by their beautiful brightly colored wings. The name of her "demoniac" species also alludes to "nympha," a word from the world of anatomy referring to the labia minora of the female genitalia. In Humbert's eyes, she furthermore has much in common both with the femme-enfant, or woman-child, figure cherished by surrealists such as André Breton, who exalted in its spontaneous innocence and connection with unconscious realms as the primary source of artistic creativity (Lolita is, after all, Humbert Humbert's muse, providing him with subject matter and inspiration) and, paradoxically, with the femme fatale, or image of woman as erotic and destructive force, the deadly temptress, fostered by nineteenth- and early twentieth-century writers and artists such as Baudelaire, Beardsley, and Proust (all significantly alluded to in the pages of Nabokov's novel). By submerging Dolly's personality in these definitions, references, and allusions, Humbert attempts to translate her into "Lolita," a being not quite human. Yet clearly he fails, for many readers find themselves able to stand free of his paradigms (surely as constrictive as those Freudian ones he mocks with such wicked relish) and glimpse for brief moments the authentic Dolly's pain and isolation.

Once again, however, things aren't quite so simple in Nabokov's universe. If, on the one hand, he gives us a vicious victimizer whom we can nonetheless come to understand, and perhaps even ultimately sympathize with, then, on the other, he also gives us a poignant victim whom we can nonetheless come to find unpleasant, even unlikable. Dolly is, all things considered, brash. She is rude. She talks back to her mother, calls her names, taunts her by throwing a tennis ball in her direction. She steals Humbert's bacon and clobbers him with a shoetree when she believes he's in cahoots with Charlotte to send Dolly to camp against her wishes. She is slothful, sarcastic, and cynical—all well before she falls under Humbert's brutal power. She suffers "fits of disorganized boredom" and "intense and vehement griping," and represents no less than the exemplary mindless American shopper: "If some café sign proclaimed Icecold Drinks, she was automatically stirred, although all drinks everywhere were ice-cold. She it was to whom ads were dedicated: the ideal consumer, the subject and object of every foul poster" (148). Moreover, she turns out to be just as much the dissembler as Humbert. Both are tainted by the theatricality of things. Both have made an art of manipulation. Both are keenly aware that they are role-playing, scripting their own lives and each other's. Dolly adores acting, jumping at the opportunity to be in Quilty's drama. A lover of overstated musicals, underworlders, and westerners, she "sees herself as a starlet" (65), and Humbert knows early on that if he tried to kiss her "she would let me do so, and even close her eyes as Hollywood teaches" (48). Suitably, then, the highlight of their second cross-country trip is their promised visit to Californian movieland, with all its glitz, glamour, and sham.

It is consequently often difficult for Humbert and us to read Dolly. Why does she (again, if we are to believe Hum's reports on the matter) early in their relationship allow Humbert to lick clean her eye into which a speck has drifted—and then to lick her other eye for no reason at all (43–44)? What are we to make of the fact that, unbidden, she throws herself into Humbert's arms and kisses him on the lips as she is about to leave for Camp Q (66)? What is her motivation when, on their way to the Enchanted Hunters, Dolly first taunts Humbert by saying he has stopped caring for her because he hasn't kissed her yet, and then "positively flow[s]" into his arms when he pulls the car over (112), or, later, before going to sleep at the hotel, again slides into his arms and acts "like the cheapest of cheap cuties" (120)? After we are told that Dolly, having learned about sex at camp from heterosexual Charlie Holmes and bisexual Elizabeth Talbot (136–37), seduces Humbert, we are given the following characteristic dialogue between them as they drive away from the hotel. Lo asks to stop at the next gas station so she can go to the washroom.

> "We shall stop wherever you want," I said. And then as a love-ly, lonely, supercilious grove . . . started to echo greenly the rush of our car, . . . I suggested we might perhaps—
> "Drive on," my Lo cried shrilly.
> "Righto. Take it easy." (Down, poor beast, down.)
> I glanced at her. Thank God, the child was smiling.
> "You chump," she said, sweetly smiling at me. "You revolting creature. I was a daisy-fresh girl, and look at what you've done to

me. I ought to call the police and tell them you raped me. Oh, you
dirty, dirty old man." (140–41)

Notice the oscillation of Dolly's tone. She begins by asking to
stop at the next restroom, indicating Humbert has hurt her during
their intercourse at the hotel that morning. Humbert immediately
agrees with her request, only thoughtlessly to suggest they stop on a
side road for one more tumble. Dolly's answer comes back "shrilly,"
her voice apparently charged with fear and frustration, and yet in the
next instant we see she's actually "sweetly smiling." She jokingly says
that Humbert, the "dirty, dirty old man" (which accusation is plainly
true enough) has just raped Dolly, a "daisy-fresh girl" (which assertion
is plainly false). Dolly has no intention of calling the police, and there
is some reason to suspect she's fine physically (although they stop in
Lepingville and buy, among other things, a box of sanitary pads, the
incident isn't brought up again). Nevertheless, both Humbert and the
reader are unclear on the extent to which Dolly is just toying with
Humbert, the extent to which she is acting to gain an excuse to call
Quilty, and the extent to which he and we should take that "ominous
hysterical note" in her voice seriously, since she has just been funning
him, and yet presumably not funning him, both at the same time.

Occasionally, then, she is painted as terribly naïve about her situation (allowing Humbert to lick her eye, for instance), occasionally
self-consciously flirtatious (the hug and kiss on the lips before and after
Camp Q), and occasionally exceedingly astute for a 12-year-old in
1940s America ("The word is incest," she tells Humbert when he
searches for the right one to describe their relationship at the hotel
[119]). In a sense, Dolly too is an artist of sorts. She learns to be an
actress to get, among other things, what she wants from Humbert
(access to Quilty and freedom from the cage into which Humbert has
locked her—putting us back, by the way, with that ape in the Jardin
des Plantes), just as Hum learns to be a spinner of fictions to get,
among other things, what he wants from her (access to the transcendent realm of art and freedom from the cage into which Time has
locked him).

The constellation of images and metaphors that gathers around Dolly highlights several of these points. Chess, to name one, comes to play an obviously important role in the novel, especially in Humbert's sadistic games with Gaston Godin; Dolly is both Hum's pitiable pawn and "formidable Queen" (182). Less apparent is the canine leitmotif, from that "meddlesome suburban dog" (36), initially sighted on Lawn Street as Humbert approaches Charlotte's house (later quite possibly the culprit causing Mr. Beale to swerve his car and hit Charlotte [102], that appropriately "old cat" [47]), to the "baptized" cocker spaniel Humbert uses to mock the Enchanted Hunters's anti-Semitic letterhead announcing NEAR CHURCHES (a coded message that only Gentiles can decipher) and NO DOGS (261). Humbert often refers to himself as a hound, and to Dolly as his pet and bitch. Dolly also enters into the leitmotif of dolls, mannequins, and puppets. These include the grotesque bald doll nursed by the repulsive 15-year-old prostitute in Paris (24); Dolly's "ballerina of wool and gauze" (45); "the two puppets" working on the distant shore of Hourglass Lake (87); the "doll-like" figures used by Beale's son in his diagram of the fatal car accident (102); Quilty, who in his convertible resembles "a display dummy" (219), and many others. Dolly is Humbert's puppet, just as all the characters are Nabokov's, just as all of us (Nabokov insinuates) are McFate's. Dolly is associated with animals besides, becoming at one time or another Humbert's colt, monkey, lamb, and bird, and is often paired with the passionate colors of crimson and pink—and more than once with the "Eden-red" apple (58) and apple-patterned dress (111) that conjure echoes of the original fall from innocence. That forbidden fruit likewise jibes nicely with the images of eating that regularly equate sex and food as Humbert first consumes Dolly with his eyes and then with his mouth.

Most famous among the book's leitmotifs is the butterfly. The avid lepidopterist Nabokov, who discovered a new species in 1941, published numerous essays on the subject, and conducted unpaid research at the American Museum of Natural History and at Harvard's Museum of Comparative Zoology (resulting in his election to the Cambridge Entomological Society in 1943). He found butterflies appealing not for their inherent beauty alone (he thought them, like people, sometimes attractive and sometimes not) but for the beauty of the chase. In *Lolita,* Nabokov's quest after the perfect butterfly meta-morphoses into Humbert's after the perfect nymphet. Often possessing the sharp eye of the scientist in his descriptions of place and person, Humbert equates himself with various predators of the butterfly, including toads, spiders, and hummingbirds. Dolly, like butterflies, adores fruit; she is a "nymph" in the entomological sense, and, as if to underscore the idea, a butterfly floats before her on the tennis court at the moment she nears a kind of Keatsian perfection (234). Moreover, numerous allusions to butterflies drift through the novel, from its fore-word, where the name John Ray, Jr., echoes that of the historical John Ray, the English naturalist who did much of his work on butterflies, to Quilty's pun ("Maeterlinck-Schmetterling" [301]) nearly 300 pages later that jokes on the German word for the insect.

This sort of metaphoric and imagistic resonance invites the read-er to conceive of Dolly as more than just one little flesh-and-blood girl. Nabokov's disgust with the term aside, we might even feel inclined to make the argument that her character approaches something akin to symbol, that literary device in which an object signifies a wide range of references beyond itself. In Humbert's eyes, as we have already noted, Dolly Haze stands for more than Dolly Haze. She stands for unattain-able perfection, for a gateway to the past, the unconscious, lost inno-cence, and the creative impulse itself. On a more pedestrian plane, her relationship with Humbert, laced as it is with bribes and blackmail and psychological brutality, and doubled with those healthier ones of Avis Byrd and her father, Mona Dahl and hers, also represents a gruesome parody of the relationship between every parent and child. Ironically, Freud is taken hyper-literally in this hyper-anti-Freudian novel; the daughter's suitors become the father's rivals in a wildly tangible way. Feminists have seen that relationship as a symbol for the male will toward dominance in our patriarchal culture. Others have seen it as a symbol of homosexual love. Dolly at 12, after all, possesses the body of a boy, and not a woman, and various mentions of gay love in the classical world, from Roman bath practices to sapphic love, abound. Gaston Godin's adoration of male nymphs, and his wall covered with photos of homosexual artists (181–82), parallels Hum's adoration of

Dolly, and his interest throughout his life with pictures of nymphets. In case we might overlook such an interpretation, Humbert reminds us that one of his psychiatrists once labeled him "potentially homosexual" (34). Of course, he predictably turns the incident into another lampoon of Freudianism, but several critics have wondered if perhaps he doth protest too much on this score.

Despite that symbolic aura aglow around her, though, Dolly continues to remain a brave little flesh-and-blood girl as well. Even in the touchstone scene in Coalmont, years after her mistreatment at the hands of Humbert (and Quilty), she exhibits courage, calm, and mature poise. Indeed, regardless of all he has done to her, Humbert can't for the life of him suppress Dolly's inherent sense of the normal. At some deep stratum of her psyche, she is able to intuit what is right and wrong in the world, refusing, for example, to partake of the "crazy things, the filthy things" her lover Quilty asked her to do at Duk Duk Ranch (277).

But she *has* changed, and in many ways changed for the worse, over the course of her stay with Hum. She begins her emotional hardening on their first cross-country trek when she starts hanging around with lowlifes, "all muscles and gonorrhea" (160). Back in school, she skirts delinquency by scrawling four-letter words in red lipstick on health pamphlets. She enters a sleazy relationship with Quilty, himself a drug user and pornographer. And, when Humbert sees her for their final meeting, she is a frazzled 17-year-old woman living in a broken-down shack. A final insult to the young spunky girl she had been, Dolly now even smokes like her mother, as "gracefully, in a blue mist, Charlotte Haze rose from the grave" (275). Married to Dick Schiller, the kind, devoted mechanic with romantic aspirations to strike out for Alaska, the last American frontier, Dolly's romantic aspirations to strike out for Hollywood and the possibility of a spectacular life there have gone the way of the blue mist. Still in love with Quilty ("he was the only man she had ever been crazy about"), she has become almost blandly indifferent toward her relationship with her husband ("Oh, Dick was a lamb, they were quite happy together") and even more so toward her past attachment with Humbert ("In her washed-out gray eyes, strangely spectacled, our poor romance was for a moment reflected, pondered upon, and dismissed like a dull party" [272]). And yet that dull party has made her what she is, brought her to this poor place.

Part of Dolly dies a metaphorical death during her odyssey with Humbert. Her youth, her vim, and her innocence perish. Unbeknown to her persecutor, real nitty-gritty death catches up with her and her baby shortly thereafter on the symbolically significant Christmas Day 1952. Humbert may fairly enough see himself as a martyr to love, but Dolly has equally (if against her will) relinquished everything to her pursuer's lust, and her innocent stillborn baby is a hauntingly fitting image for the hope and happiness and childhood she has sacrificed. Even though her small-scale story takes place in good part in a quiet green corner of northeastern America at a point in history when the larger globe is in the process of scrabbling noisily out of the ruins of the megalithic World War II, with its tens of millions of abominable lives and abominable deaths, Nabokov proposes that Dolly's life and death, the life and death of every individual, remain important.

CHARLOTTE HAZE AND THE AMERICAN DAYMARE

Exploring the complex characters of Humbert and Dolly, we discover much to weigh and wonder about, much to sympathize with, empathize with, and try to understand. Humbert's second wife and Dolly's mother, Charlotte Haze, on the other hand, is a secondary player in the novel who provides us with little to contemplate and even less to feel for. She is, to a large degree, the incarnation of *poshlost,* a Russian term Nabokov often applied to items, ideas, and people with fiendish derision. The various nuances of *poshlost* include "corny trash, vulgar clichés, Philistinism in all its phases, imitations of imitations, bogus profundities, crude moronic and dishonest pseudo-literature" (*SO,* 101). Coming close to the American notion of kitsch, *poshlost* connotes trashy art, false sentimentality, and fake refinement, and hence opposes originality, individuality, and sincere cultivation.

Charlotte is *poshlost* personified. She is kindred spirit to those vacuous women in e. e. cummings's poem, "the Cambridge ladies who live in furnished souls," who sport "comfortable minds" and beliefs in "Christ and Longfellow, both dead." Charlotte inhabits a house whose front hall is indicatively clogged with "a white-eyed wooden thingamabob of commercial Mexican origin" alongside "that banal darling of the arty middle class, van Gogh's 'Arlésienne'" (36). She is the kind of person who sprinkles her sentences with forced French and Italian phrases and "whose polished words may reflect a book club or bridge club, or any other deadly conventionality, but never her soul." She lacks an ounce of genuine humor, is "utterly indifferent at heart to the dozen or so possible subjects of a parlor conversation, but very particular about the rules of such conversations" (37). All form and no content, she is as cloying over an indifferent Humbert as Humbert is over an indifferent Dolly, but, unlike the cultivated European, this brash American is also a middle-class conformist with an overblown sense of her own sophistication. She is gullible, vulgar, partial to scotch, slow-witted, domineering, and a woman who mistakenly perceives herself as a sensuous individual.

In addition, she is jealous and hateful of Dolly. Filling out a questionnaire at the back of *A Guide to Your Child's Development,* she underlines 10 negative epithets for her child ("aggressive," "listless," and "obstinate" among them) and leaves the 30 positive ones untouched (81). Although Hum and she only cohabit for a fast 50 days in 1947, that time is more than enough for harried Hum, who tends to dehumanize her with the tag "the Haze woman" and who, when perfunctorily making love to her, dreams of his Lolita. The devilish icing on her character's cake is that Nabokov names her after the poetic yet practical heroine of Wolfgang von Goethe's mawkish eighteenth-century romantic novella, *Sorrows of Young Werther.* There, Goethe's Charlotte marries another man, driving love-smitten Werther after much sighing and crying to suicide. Something near the inverse happens in *Lolita.*

Perhaps more interesting about this silly woman whom Humbert labels everything from a monkey to a clumsy seal, an octopus to a big bitch, is that she leads us into a serious consideration of the author's vision of America itself. A number of early critics, particularly those in Britain and France, found Nabokov's first American novel in subject matter and feel an attack upon his new homeland. "This is something that pains me considerably more than the idiotic accusation of immorality," Nabokov countered in his afterword (315). He repeated this view in his *Playboy* interview: "I am annoyed when the glad news is spread that I am ridiculing America" (*SO*, 32). In a 1969 interview with the *New York Times*, social upheaval after social upheaval rolling across the land, he anachronistically affirmed that "America is the only country where I feel mentally and emotionally at home" (*SO*, 131). In another, published three years before, he answered when asked if he considered himself an American: "Yes, I do. I am as American as April in Arizona. . . . I do feel a suffusion of warm, lighthearted pride when I show my green USA passport at European frontiers. Crude criticism of American affairs offends and distresses me" (*SO*, 98).

Nabokov's nigh-patriotic sense of his newfound home is highlighted by Humbert's fine and fastidious attention to the details of American landscape and mentions of the United States as "the country of rosy children and great trees, where life would be such an improvement on dull dingy Paris" (27), "the lovely, trustful, dreamy, enormous country" (176) whose wilds retain "a quality of wide-eyed, unsung, innocent surrender that my lacquered, toy-bright Swiss villages and exhaustively lauded Alps no longer possess" (168). In light of this, the double cross-country odysseys of discovery on which Dolly and Humbert embark, prefigured by that map of the United States he comes across in the *Young People's Encyclopedia* (51), and reminiscent of those quests in such American classics as Mark Twain's *Huck Finn* and Jack Kerouac's *On the Road,* are no less than epic catalogs and epic celebrations of the pluralistic particulars that shape the United States, filled with Whitmanesque litanies of motel monikers, tourist sites, tennis courts, picnic areas, gas stations, restrooms, diners, coast-to-coast geographies, place names, and the flora and fauna that constitute the rich "crazy quilt of forty-eight states" (152).[8] Furthermore, Humbert's adoration of America only seems amplified by his downright "allergic" reaction to "the Old and rotting World" (91), "sweet, mellow, rotting Europe" (281).

Once again, however, we must learn to trust the tale and not the teller. After all, who are among our major representatives of this lovely, trustful, dreamy, enormous country but brash Charlotte and crass Dolly? While it is true that Humbert thinks of himself as a decadent European debaucher of robust American innocence, the novel itself actually complicates this idea. In a sense, Dolly's buoyant sparkle seduces Humbert, that genetic amalgam of all of sweet, mellow, rotting Europe, making the book's subject also how weak, elderly Europe is tempted by young, Philistine America. We should remember, too, that Humbert is no longer technically a European, but a brand-new American citizen, and that the most morally corrupt character in the book, Clare Quilty, is not from the Riviera at all, but New Jersey.

Nor is Nabokov's the wholly idyllic view of the American landscape that he might have us believe. If we look a little more closely, we see that roadside U.S.A. is littered with Frigid Queens, hunchbacks, the kitschy culture of U-Beam Cottages and Buck's-and-Doe's restroom signs, Columbus's flagship aswarm with monkeys in an Indiana zoo, and "pickaninnies who will . . . tap-dance for pennies" in New Orleans (156). The only ART in the course of Hum and Dolly's trip turns out to be the initials for the American Refrigerator Transit Company (157). Moreover, if a man tries to enjoy this "idyllic" landscape with his sweetheart, "poisonous plants burn his sweetheart's buttocks, nameless insects sting his; sharp items of the forest floor prick his knees, insects hers; and all around there abides a sustained rustle of potential snakes" (168). Again, below the lovely ideal lurks the immensely disagreeable real.

This basic structure of positive-appearance-of-surfaces versus negative-reality-of-depths goes a long way toward typifying the novel's ultimate sense of the United States. At first glance, we view a Norman Rockwell portrait of shady green suburbs atwinkle with children's laughter. But as we read on we find ourselves stepping through the gilt-framed looking glass into the dark geography of David Lynch's film *Blue Velvet*. Beneath the bucolic beats the bestial. Nabokov's depictions of characters like sick Clare Quilty, uncouth Charlotte, coarse Dolly, depraved Gaston Godin, brainless Miss Pratt, and racist John Farlow, show us the underbelly of American consciousness. The leitmotifs of anti-Semitism (Humbert is mistaken for a Jew at least three times; hotels hint they are for Gentiles only) and racism (Charlotte's concerns about Humbert's racial purity; John Farlow's snipes at Italians and African Americans) serve to emphasize the point.

Moreover, Humbert Humbert's actions indict not only him, but a whole society. Intentionally or not, Nabokov has written a kind of Swiftean "Modest Proposal" for the second half of the twentieth century, a how-to pamphlet for the American mind searching for fulfillment. If *Lolita* is a novel about the quest for the American dream (embodied by Dolly herself), it is also one that shows us just how easily the desire for that dream can replace warmth and caring with lust and obsession. The compassionate consummation of love transmogrifies into its capitalist commodification. Such a perspective places this umber-toned comedy in the satiric tradition of Nathanael West's scathing raids against the American psyche launched from books like *Miss Lonelyhearts* and *Day of the Locust* (interestingly enough, Nabokov was once asked to adapt the latter to the screen). As in William Carlos Williams's poem "To Elsie," in *Lolita* America has gone crazy. There is no one to drive the car of state. Or, much worse, it turns out there is a madman behind the wheel.

CLARE QUILTY AND DOUBLE TROUBLE

Aside from that quick allusion to Vivian Darkbloom's biography, *My Cue,* mentioned by John Ray, Jr., in his foreword, and that "bubble of hot poison," which appears in chapter 5, part 1, only to burst on Cue's lips as he dies in chapter 36, part 2, we initially encounter Quilty in chapter 8. Apparently on a whim, Humbert transcribes part of a page from *Who's Who in the Limelight,* a book he comes across in the prison library. On that page is the playwright's biography. But during our first reading of Nabokov's novel, we probably quickly forget him and the fact that he was born in 1911, one year after Hum, in Ocean City, just as Hum was near another large body of water on the Riviera. We forget that he is author of such provocatively entitled dramas as

Little Nymph, Fatherly Love, and *Dark Age,* and we forget that among his hobbies are, suitably enough, fast cars, photography, and pets. We probably even forget that the first name of the actress whose brief biography follows Quilty's in *Who's Who* is, sure enough, Dolores, that she was born (like Dolly) in the midwest, and that she appeared in a drama called, yes, *The Murdered Playwright.*

We encounter traces of Quilty a host of subtle times over the course of the next several hundred pages: from his Uncle Ivor who practices dentistry in Ramsdale to that photo of the fellow smoking Dromes in Dolly's room; from his signature phallic red convertible at the Enchanted Hunters (passionate and devilish red is Quilty's color) to the "car changing its shape mirage-like in the surface glare" on the road behind the couple as they strike out across America (153); from the mysterious man on the other end of the line—to whom Dolly is speaking when Humbert discovers her in a phone booth after she has left their Beardsley house in a huff—to the increasingly frequent references to the person who resembles Hum's Swiss uncle, Gustave Trapp. But even after Dolly finally names him for Humbert in Coalmont, Quilty remains a naught for us. Instead of sharing the scoundrel's actual appellation with the reader, Humbert gives us only a bantam hint, the word "waterproof" (272), alluding to a scene 183 pages earlier when Jean Farlow *almost* mentions him in passing. Not until we are roaming through Pavor Manor with Humbert during the novel's conclusion do most of us finally put together the puzzling pieces that are our cues to Cue. No wonder, then, that Hum dubs his antagonist Clare the Impredictable and, even more to the point, Clare Obscure.

When those pieces finally do fall together, they reveal a sleazy cocaine and heroin user and amoral pornographer who has much in common with such nineteenth-century decadents as Joris Karl Huysmans in France and (a name that figures prominently in *Lolita*) Aubrey Beardsley in England in their experiments into extremes of sensation and in their attacks on the social and moral standards of their day. Although he is the only man Dolly is ever crazy about (an example of her own sense of *poshlost,* America's blindness to hard realities), cool Quilty captures her only to play a glib game; once that game has been played out, dispensing with her is a breeze. After Dolly refuses to perform fellatio on some of his fellow degenerates at Duk Duk Ranch ("she used, in all insouciance really, a disgusting slang term which, in a literal French translation, would be *souffler*," Humbert explains [277]), Quilty simply gives her the boot, casting her alone into the world. There, after several years of wandering and waitressing, she will meet her future husband Richard Schiller and her life will devolve into the one Humbert uncovers in that Coalmont home. If Humbert's dominant mode of perception is the photograph (recall all the times he refers to them, from the one his aunt takes of Annabel, to those of the girl-children he notices on the walls of Camp Q, to the sharp and beautifully contoured linguistic snapshots he creates of his Lolita on various tennis courts), then Quilty's dominant mode of perception is the bad blue movie. Humbert's obsession with pristine and transcendental photographic moments links him to the romantic quest for Keatsian perfection. Quilty's obsession with tacky pornographic flicks links him to the commercial quest for kinky perversity. Cue's mode of perception even debases the already-debased vision of artifice and capital perpetuated by Hollywood.

And yet, from a slightly different vantage point, Quilty's infamous films aren't so extremely dissimilar from Humbert's erotic prose. Not, that is, if we were to strip away all of Humbert's gorgeous courtly poetry from it. In other words, those fetid films form a kind of mirror image of that pleasing prose. This observation leads us directly into one of the major themes of the novel: that of the double. True enough, Quilty sometimes takes on the resonance of a conventionally round character, complex in temperament and capable of surprising us, and this is the point of view from which we have just been discussing him. More often, however, he takes on the metaphoric resonance of Humbert's dark self, embodying, as it were, Humbert's unsound psychology. From this point of view, Quilty joins the long literary tradition of the doppelgänger (German for "double goer"), or the mysterious double, that includes such notable and fitting examples as Poe's "William Wilson," Wilde's *The Picture of Dorian Gray,* and Conrad's "The Secret Sharer."

The similarities between Humbert and Quilty are striking. Humbert flirts with the idea of growing a toothbrush mustache, while

Quilty actually sports one. Both possess similar bathrobes and hairy hands, and both are almost the same age. Humbert refers to Quilty as his "uncle" (123), "brother" (247), "shadow" (215), "another Humbert" (217), and even overtly as his "double" (236). Just as Oedipus finds another side of himself when he, the first detective of them all, quests after the cause of all the troubles in Thebes, so too does Humbert Humbert find another side of himself when he, a sleuth on the cryptogrammic paper chase, quests after the cause of all his troubles in the maze that is America. Just as Dolly can't read "the hideous hieroglyphics of [Humbert's] fatal lust" (78), so too Humbert has difficulty reading the hieroglyphics seeded (or at least *possibly* seeded) across the United States by Quilty, who in many ways takes on the role of McFate himself by toying with and tormenting unsuspecting Humbert and innocent Dolly. Hence it is fair to say that along his journey Humbert discovers his enemy half, his perverse alter ego, one Clare Quilty, who is clearly guilty of stealing his hopes and dreams, "Quine the Swine" (32), that satanic component of Humbert that has, in a sense, overwhelmed his personality and that he must destroy to regain something like balance. It is possibly for this reason that Humbert never shows contrition for killing Quilty, less character than metaphor for that aspect of Humbert's psyche responsible for ruining Lolita's life. Quilty's death becomes a psychological and moral rite of purification.

Nabokov warns us not to take Quilty-as-rounded-character too seriously by emphasizing the comic elements of his murder. His demise at Pavor (Latin for "panic" or "terror") Manor on the nicely named Grimm Road both nods appreciatively toward and burlesques Poe's grim House of Usher (both in setting and in theme of incest), the ominous castles of fairy tales, and the Gothic ambiance of much late eighteenth-century fiction with its brooding, magic, and mystery. But the violence of this unforgettable scene takes on an almost cartoonish cast. Quilty, by way of purgation, must recite bad poetry and, though threatened and then shot repeatedly, finds time to tempt Humbert with explorer and psychoanalyst Melanie Weiss's collection of photos documenting more than 800 male organs; play the piano; dance like Nijinski; ascend a flight of stairs; take a brief inventory of his abode;

and snuggle among bedclothes in his master bedroom before dying, "a big pink bubble with juvenile connotations" (304) upon his lips. The scene is part Hollywood knock-down, drag-out tussle ("elderly readers will surely recall at this point the obligatory scene in the Westerns" [299]), part Shakespearean revenge tragedy (replete with insanity, a scheming villain, long death throes, bloody on-stage murder, and even mention of the Bard himself with a punny allusion to *Macbeth* [301]), and part Keatonesque slapstick, at the level of both action and language (the wacky wrestling, the awful Eliotic verse, the puns, Quilty's fake British accent and monologue riddled with non-sequiturish pleas for Humbert to drop Chum, his gun).

Nor is the doubling between Humbert and Quilty enough. At the instant we begin to take this psychological theme seriously, the author begins to veritably saturate the text with doubles, with doubles of doubles, until we begin to realize that he's as much parodying as embracing that literary tradition of the doppelgänger. We thereby come to understand that Nabokov disturbs the easy duality between good and evil suggested by the double, proposing that the situation is much more complicated than those of us raised in the strictly binary system of Western morality might imagine. While it would be virtually impossible (as well as tedious) to catalog all occurrences of this theme, a brief laundry list might serve to represent the whole. Cue is himself doubled by three other characters in the novel. First is Humbert's real uncle, Trapp, his father's homosexual cousin; this reinforces the gay leitmotif running through the book. Second is Humbert's fellow chess player and neighborhood pederast, Gaston Godin; this reinforces both the gay leitmotif and underscores Humbert/Quilty's "depraved" sexual nature. Third is Dolly's classmate Kenneth Knight, the boy who exhibits himself to whomever he can whenever he can; this reinforces both Humbert/Quilty's "depraved" sexual nature and underscores the leitmotifs of voyeurism and exhibitionism that run through the text. The name John Ray, Jr., (J.R./Jr.) suggests doubleness, as of course does the double rumble within Humbert Humbert (and his three other aliases: Otto Otto, Mesmer Mesmer, and Lambert Lambert) and the alliteration within those of Clare Quilty, Vanessa van Ness, Gaston Godin, Harold Haze, Bill Brown, Clarence Clark, and so on. There are no fewer than four sets of twins or siblings in Dolly's class, the township of Soda contains a mirrory 1001 people, Humbert dreams of Dolly's child making it big in the stutter-year 2020, Rita's name rhymes with Lolita's, and the name of the person who owns the house where Humbert first beholds Dolly-as-nymphet is "Haze," while the name of the person who owns the motor court where Humbert last beholds Dolly-as-nymphet is "Hays." Humbert's relationship with Dolly is mate to his relationship with Annabel, Dolly's shrewdness duplicates Humbert's, Valeria dies in childbirth in 1945 as does Dolly in 1952, Humbert and Dolly's second sojourn across America reiterates their first, Quilty's Pavor Manor darkly repeats Charlotte Haze's middle-class castle, and the novel's afterword matches its foreword. At one point Humbert accuses Dolly of "playing a double game" (243), but clearly the same could be said with even more accuracy about Nabokov.

A key image reinforcing the text's sense of repetition is the mirror. It appears as early as chapter 11, as Humbert and Dolly stand before the one in Charlotte's bedroom and Humbert licks out the particle that has drifted into his darling's eye. But it returns again and again, culminating in the delightfully surreal description of the couple's room at the Enchanted Hunters: "There was a double bed, a mirror, a double bed in the mirror, a closet door with mirror, a bathroom door ditto, a blue-dark window, a reflected bed there, the same in the closet mirror, two chairs, a glass-topped table, two bedtables, a double bed: a big panel bed, to be exact, with a Tuscan rose chenille spread, and two frilled, pink-shaded nightlamps, left and right" (119). Under the hyperbolic humor beats a serious sense of claustrophobia, entrapment, circumscribing obsession—one more (and perhaps the most important) prison in a book full of them. Here we encounter "the mirror you break your nose against" (225), solipsism.

From the Latin words *solus* ("alone") and *ipse* ("self"), solipsism denotes any doctrine attaching primary importance to the self. It may simply refer to a radical version of self-seeking associated with egoism, or it may, taken to its logical extreme, refer to a metaphysical belief that the self is the whole of existence, the world and the objects in it nothing save inventions of mind. We can track this second variety back to Descartes's famous pronouncement, *cogito ergo sum,* or "I think, therefore I am" (though it is helpful to remember that the French philosopher ultimately rejected solipsistic doubt as overblown and foolish). Humbert Humbert embraces both the self-seeking and metaphysical versions of the notion, piggy-backing Nabokov himself, who believed that reality is "one of the few words which mean nothing without quotes" (312), that it is "a very subjective affair," and that "you can get nearer and nearer, so to speak, to reality; but you never get near enough because reality is an infinite succession of steps, levels of perception, false bottoms, and hence unquenchable, unattainable" (*SO,* 10–11).

Humbert takes these slightly skeptical premises to their wholly ridiculous and dangerous extremes by misreading and mishandling Dolly to the extent that, finally, he feels he has "safely solipsized" her (60): "What I had madly possessed was not she, but my own creation, another, fanciful Lolita—perhaps more real than Lolita; overlapping, encasing her; floating between me and her, and having no will, no consciousness—indeed, no life of her own" (62). He realizes from the start, then, that he dehumanizes her by transforming this flesh-and-blood girl into little more than a projection of his own skewed psyche. And this comes as no shock to either him or us, since Hum's propensity for a solipsistic view of the universe dates from the days of his youth. In that snapshot taken by his Aunt Sybil of Annabel, her parents, Dr. Cooper, and Humbert relaxing around a table in a sidewalk café, young Hum can be seen "sitting somewhat apart from the rest," "a moody, beetle-browed boy," "looking away" (13). Among the interests he and Annabel share are "the plurality of inhabited worlds, competitive tennis, infinity, solipsism" (12). The sexual fantasies in which he soon engages with little girls while perching on park benches pretending to read are nothing if not emblems of a self-absorbed soul.

One man's solipsism, it nearly goes without saying, is another's psychosis. By the time Humbert and Quilty enact their dream-exchange at the Enchanted Hunters, the former preparing to deflower his darling, the novel shrugs off its patina of traditional realism and reveals the increasingly hallucinatory machinations of an erratic mind in extremis. And by the time Humbert and Dolly begin their first cross-country tour, we understand that the journey will not be so much into the heart of America (though it will surely be that) as it will be deeper and deeper into the heart of an intensely isolated consciousness. In this dingy light, the mazy cryptogrammic paper chase becomes an objective correlative for the involutions of Hum's deformed psyche projected onto a whole country; as we drive away from the Enchanted Hunters, we literally cross a base border into umber and black Humberland where the only language spoken is "Humbertish" (35).

This movement from the representation of external reality to the representation of internal reality accounts for the incremental presence of the grotesque in the novel. The launchpoint occurs shortly after Humbert's fall from grace with Annabel, as he starts visiting those eerie Parisian prostitutes, and soon the text's tendency toward the bizarre and abnormal escalates into a legion of misshapen and nightmarish characters, objects, and landscapes. Examples are the "old invalid Miss Opposite" in her "brand new wheel chair" (50) and Dolly's classmates, like "Grace and her ripe pimples" and "Ginny and her lagging leg" (53); the refrigerator that "roared at [Humbert] viciously while [he] removed the ice from its heart" (96) and the fire hydrant at the scene of Charlotte's death that joins the ranks of "nightmare cripples" (106); the "hairy hermaphrodite" that troubles Humbert's dreams on his way to pick up Dolly at Camp Q (109) and the "accursed truck," "its backside carbuncles pulsating" that Humbert finds himself behind as he drives Dolly toward their first tryst (116). It is thus with good reason that Humbert refers to the couple's trip as "our grotesque journey" (229), populated as it is with that "hunchbacked and hoary Negro in a uniform of sorts" who waits on Dolly and Hum at their first hotel (117); the elderly man "with a broken nose" who wipes their windshield clean in a roadside gas station (141); the "mummy-necked farmer" they pass in Kansas (152); the "three horrible Boschian cripples" among whom Dolly one day plays tennis (235); the "naked girl, with cinnabar nipples and indigo delta, charmingly tattooed on the back of [Frank's, Mrs. Hays's beau's] crippled hand" (245)—all climaxing with Quilty's gruesomely drawn-out death.

The Moral Dimension: Umber and Black Humberland

One way to view the novel, therefore, is as the chronicle of yet another and certainly the most massive mental breakdown in Humbert's life. The narrative's change in atmosphere from fastidious realism to distorted surreality marks Hum's last descent into insanity. He warns us of as much in the journal he keeps at Charlotte's when he comments that "I shall probably have another breakdown if I stay any longer in this house, under the strain of this intolerable temptation" (47). But that intolerable temptation is only one in a series of dramatic strains weighing on Hum's fragile psychology. The pressure of Charlotte's death is soon added, then his and Dolly's flight from Camp Q and Ramsdale, a list of frightening near-discoveries during the course of their trysts, their awareness of the mounting suspicions of Miss Pratt and others about them, Quilty's tormenting appearance, Dolly's final July Fourth escape in 1949, Humbert's subsequent July-through-November attempt to retrace his steps (culminating in his return to Beardsley and the near-murder of the wrong man, Professor Riggs), his mental collapse in the winter of 1949 and spring of 1950, his brief return to the Canadian sanatorium, his two years of anguish and alcoholism traveling with his Lolita-substitute, Rita, that last haunting meeting with Dolly in Coalmont in 1952, his killing of Quilty, his arrest, and his ensuing imprisonment.

No wonder he experiences "static" (118) when trying to talk to the man at the front desk at the Enchanted Hunters and to Quilty later on the night of his first intercourse with Dolly; that his doctor, apparently worried about his mental condition, prescribes purple placebos in place of real sleeping pills; that Hum develops a nervous tic that Dolly is the first to make sport of; that a sense of paranoia overwhelms him; and that fully realized, realistic scenes soon slide into fantastic fragmented visions, as when Humbert, returning one day with cold drinks from the hotel where they've been staying to the tennis courts where Dolly and a female companion have been playing, notices his little lover disappearing into nearby bushes with a large Cue-ish man. Hum pursues, but, he says, "as I was crashing through the shrubbery I saw, in an alternate vision, as if life's course constantly branched, Lo, in slacks, and her [female] companion, in shorts, trudging up and down a small weedy area, and beating bushes with their rackets in listless search for their last lost ball" (163). It is unsurprising that in his "mental daze" (110) he gradually has the "odd sense of living in a brand new, mad new dream world, where everything is permissible" (133).

Back once more to that cage at the Jardin des Plantes, which this time we might read as a metaphor for Humbert's mental state. He is confined by his own egoism and solipsistic consciousness, trapped in the cell of his mind. The best he can do during his confession is draw the bars to his psychological stockade, which warps and slants his view of the world. This fact helps account for the proliferation of prisons in a text obsessed with the inability of a human being to escape the compass of his limited, distorted, and dangerous perspective. Dolly is figuratively and literally held in Humbert's hoosegow, as is Quilty at the end in Pavor Manor. But we should also recall that Humbert is enthralled by Dolly, Charlotte, Quilty, the state, and even the past from which he tries to free himself by rewriting and righting the misfire of his childhood romance with Annabel. If we think of Nabokov's book in these terms, it becomes a novel about the difficulties we all experience trying to break out of the confines of our consciousnesses, out of our own solipsism, out of our self-seeking egoism, and about the difficulties we all experience trying to learn to connect and communicate with other people, to empathize with and to love them, and, at last, to break through from what we imagine another person could, or should, or might be into what they actually are. In this search for honest and moral freedom and humane acceptance, Nabokov succeeds where Humbert cannot.

LAUGHTER IN THE DARK: *LOLITA*'S COMIC VISION

We thus arrive one last time on the gilded doorstep of moral interpretation. The English writer Martin Amis hints at as much when, speaking of the differences between James Joyce, Nabokov's high modernist counterpart, and Nabokov himself, he asserts that "Joyce seemed to be cruising about on all surfaces at once, and maddeningly indulged his trick shots on high-pressure points—his drop smash, his sidespun half-volley lob. Nabokov just went out there and did the business, all litheness, power, and touch."[9] Joyce, it appears to Amis, foregrounded style and invention while backgrounding moral and psychological complexity; for Nabokov, the opposite is the case. It is easy enough, needless to say, to take exception (as we shortly shall) with the implication that Nabokov never indulged in trick shots on high-pressure points. But, be that as it may, it is true enough that his work in *Lolita* feels to many readers a good deal more emotionally rich and morally rewarding than Joyce's cooler labor in *Ulysses,* and certainly more so than the Irishman's cerebral shenanigans in *Finnegans Wake.* In part this is because Nabokov's narrative universe seems less pyrotechnically fancy, more psychically full, and more existentially resonant than Joyce's.

One of the reasons that *Lolita,* a book famous for its delicate tightrope walk between perversion and nympholepsy on the one hand and normalcy and love on the other, is so powerful is that Humbert Humbert's humor only partially covers the great despair rumbling through his heart. Beneath his witty style, beneath his dark jokes and bright puns, we sense a deadly seriousness—and often the very seriousness of death itself. Remember, just for a moment, how many people expire in the course of Humbert's tale. Humbert himself, obviously. And Dolly, Charlotte, and Quilty. But also Annabel of typhus, Valeria in childbirth, Humbert Humbert's mother by lightning, Dolly's baby and possibly Valeria's, Harold Haze and his mother, Dolly's oft-forgotten blond brother at two, Jean Farlow of cancer, Charlie Holmes in Korea, possibly Gaston Godin in Europe, and the barber's son in the town near Chestnut Court. Add to these the animal in Charlotte's basement and others along the road to which Dolly is only too happy to draw Humbert's attention, and we have a text virtually bursting with breakdown and doom. McFate, Humbert's cosmic nemesis who stands for all that can go wrong in life, makes his first apt appearance smack in the middle of Dolly's innocent class roster, then swoops down repeatedly on cringing Humbert and myriad other unsuspecting victims. During the run of things, that devilish entity transforms from Aubrey (a name neatly connecting him to the nineteenth-century decadent, Beardsley) McFate into Clare Quilty himself, the ultimate symbol of a malign creation.

Thomas Pynchon, one of Nabokov's students at Cornell, remarked almost exactly 30 years after the initial publication of *Lolita* that "when we speak of 'serious' fiction ultimately we are talking about an attitude toward death—how characters may act in its presence, for example, or how they handle it when it isn't so immediate." At the center of such writing is the recognition that "certain processes, not only thermodynamic ones but also those of a medical nature, can often not be reversed. Sooner or later we all find this out, from the inside."[10] These words strike to the essence of *Lolita*. If we read those first two pages of the foreword by John Ray, Jr., and keep them in mind as we push on, death seems to hover above every word Humbert writes. And yet surprisingly, *Lolita* remains, despite (or perhaps because of) its deep awareness of mortality and wickedness in the world, a touchingly funny text. We frequently find ourselves laughing aloud at its absurd situations, its bizarrely comical characters, and its brilliantly ambidextrous language. Within its magnificently crafted paragraphs, the man who loved movies by Laurel and Hardy, Buster Keaton, Harold Lloyd, Charlie Chaplin, and the Marx Brothers embraces a wide variety of heartfelt humor. "Human beings laugh, if you notice," Amis continues, "to express relief, exasperation, stoicism, hysteria, embarrassment, disgust, and cruelty. *Lolita* is perhaps the funniest novel in the language, because it allows laughter its full complexity and range" (Amis, 119).

From its opening sentences, we become conscious of the book's abundance of mischievously scrumptious puns, portmanteau words, neologisms, and other deft linguistic gaming. "And where are you parked, my car pet?" asks Humbert in his poem to Dolly (256), while "daymares" replace nightmares (254) and "earwitnesses" eyewitnesses (145). Even minute details elicit readerly smiles. People don't wash their cars in Nabokov's solar system, but rather "water" them (179), and a simple P.O., or post office, at Elphinstone has tucked within it references to Edgar Allan Poe (P.O.E.), elves and the fairy tale motif, and the town where Humbert will lose his own "elf," herself a pixie from Pisky (222). Such luxuriant verbal texture, plain dizzying at times owing to its creation of an optical effect whereby the reader's eye is drawn away from world and toward word, extends, sometimes to a greater degree, and sometimes to a lesser, right up to the most lyrical and emotionally poignant paragraph in the entire novel, its last, where neither Humbert nor Nabokov can restrain themselves. Their final deeply felt advice for lost Lolita? "Be true to your Dick" (309).

Such linguistic slapstick finds its analog in more physical forms. There is, for instance, the egregious sort that surfaces in Quilty's murder scene, rife with Keatonesque pratfalls, a Keystone Kop-ish chase, and a Three Stooges–like scuffle, or the already-mentioned prevalence of grotesques. Humbert himself is also a kind of cosmic double-take artist, both in the sense that he is gullible and forever surprised about so much concerning America, Dolly, and love, and in the sense that he forever causes us, his readers, to look twice in order to catch his (and behind him Nabokov's) self-reflexive tours de force—those meta-Humbertian jokes planted in Dolly's class catalog, in that excerpt from *Who's Who in the Limelight,* or in that multitude of hotel registers along that cryptogrammic paper chase. We delight in his ironic sallies: the distance between Miss Pratt's dullness in her observation that Dolly "is a lovely child, but the onset of sexual maturing seems to give her trouble" and the painful reality of Dolly's situation (193), or the more tenderly sad space that opens between Humbert's assertion that "in its published form, this book is being read, I assume, in the first years of 2000 A.D. (1935 plus eighty or ninety, live long my love)" and the reader's understanding that Dolly is already almost dead (299). We enjoy his parodic volleys: the transformation of Shakespeare's woeful "tomorrow and tomorrow and tomorrow" (*Macbeth* 5.7.19) into Quilty's capitalistic "to borrow and to borrow and to borrow" (301), the pompous academic diction of John Ray, Jr., or the fiendish fiddling with T. S. Eliot's poem, "Ash Wednesday," which bruises the Anglican anglophile's "Because I do not hope to turn again / Because I do not hope / Because I do not hope to turn" into vengeful Humbert's "Because you took advantage of a sinner / because you took advantage / because you took / because you took advantage of my disadvantage . . ." (299).

"Satire is a lesson," Nabokov once declared, "parody a game" (*SO,* 75). If so, then much of *Lolita* leans toward parody, toward the imitation of and funning with a long list of serious literature in terms of both style (that overly repetitious and severe Eliot poem, for example) and subject matter (from Roman poet Catullus's lovesick lyrics to that death speech by Macbeth) for no other reason than straightforward diabolic enjoyment and a nod-nod-wink-wink display of wit. Yet satire, the more moral and pointed form of humor, whose goal is to deride human institutions and even humanity itself in order to improve them, also visits Nabokov's novel often. We need only remember Humbert's (and Nabokov's) sarcastic barbs at everything from racism and anti-Semitism to vacuous American teen rituals and simple-minded progressive schools, this last embodied so devilishly well by Miss Pratt, who during her first interview with Humbert gets his name wrong, botches the color of Dolly's eyes, and blithely asserts that Gaston Godin is a genius. Such revelations about her intellectual denseness pave the way for her pronouncement that Beardsley School is unconcerned with having its pupils become "bookworms or be able to reel off all the capitals of Europe which nobody knows anyway." Heaven forbid. Its goal is rather to "stress the four D's: Dramatics, Dance, Debating and Dating" (177). But the ultimate satiric thrust of *Lolita* is aimed at much larger game: all those limited consciousnesses inhabiting the world, which, like Humbert Humbert, Charlotte, and Quilty, fail to grant genuine autonomy and liberty to other human beings.

In his eccentric study of the nineteenth-century Russian writer Nikolai Gogol, Nabokov comments that a single letter separates the *comic* from the *cosmic*.[11] In *Lolita* the two are inextricably bound. While funniness frequently functions at a topical level in the novel, a portmanteau word here, a parodic punch there, behind the specifics exists a much more ubiquitous comic vision that emphasizes, as Dolly concludes near the end of her life, that "this world was just one gag after another" (273). Such an optic views existence through the darkly tinted glasses of black humor, a primarily postwar brand associated with such novels as Günter Grass's *The Tin Drum,* Joseph Heller's *Catch-22,* and Kurt Vonnegut's *Slaughter-House Five* that evinces an existentially bitter tone and fantastically morbid situations peopled by baleful or inept characters who maneuver through a nightmarish pluriverse. Like Humbert, those characters are exiles, and, like Humbert, they have been cast adrift on the unpredictable sea of McFated absurdity, their religious and transcendental mooring lines snapped. The result for Nabokov's narrator is the uneasy if unprovable feeling that "life is a joke," and the desperate attempt to belie that feeling by making cosmos out of chaos through "the melancholy and very local palliative of articulate art" (283).

But the articulate art he creates is much less stable than he might wish it to be. While Humbert longs to immortalize his love for Dolly in language, the language he sculpts also happens to immortalize his crimes, his rampant immorality, even his ability to jest at the most somber and inappropriate moments, thereby throwing his definition of love, not to mention the seriousness of his objectives, into question. The consequences of this, according to Lionel Trilling's evaluation, are the novel's main interests: "its ambiguity of tone . . . and its ambiguity of intention, its ability to arouse uneasiness, to throw the reader off balance, to require him to change his stances and shift his position and move on."[12] In other words, just as *Lolita* challenges its readers to judge Humbert, only to subvert or severely complicate the act of judgment by building sympathy for him as he slowly gains awareness of himself and his deeds, so too does it challenge a starkly serious interpretation by building into its very structure a shape-shifting comedy that interrogates stark seriousness itself.

This Mobius-strip of a narrative gesture is deconstructive to the extent that it undoes the moral authority of the text at the instant it asserts it. *Lolita* hence constructs as it destructs, dismantling the mechanisms of univocal interpretation and problematizing the exact idea of morality we have heretofore been exploring. The effect is the appearance of a polyphonic mode of narration that foregrounds uncertainty, instability, and incongruity. Not unlike the medieval Feast of Fools, as Richard Pearce observes, Nabokov's text exhibits a diabolical strategy that demolishes psychological and social orders and leaves absolutes dangling: "in the end the world is turned upside down, order is destroyed, reality is undermined by a comic force that is at once threatening and enlivening." Nabokov's impulse, thus, "is to create a recognizable world and then undermine or deconstruct every possible vantage from which we might form judgments. In the end he leaves us with a rich and tantalizing verbal surface suspended, as it were, over a black hole."[13] Perhaps an overstatement, we think, until we recall that Humbert Humbert makes much the same point when, at the beginning of his life story, he notes that rational analysis of his motives and actions soon surrenders to an imaginative impulse that "feeds the analytic faculty with boundless alternatives and . . . causes each visualized route to fork and re-fork without end in the maddeningly complex prospect of my past" (13). As in "The Garden of Forking Paths," that famous short fiction by magical realist Jorge Luis Borges, pathways of knowing divide and redivide, branch and web, into a giddily intricate network of possibilities, perspectives, and purposes, erasing the hopeful chance of rigid reading while entering the anteroom of postmodernism's radical relativity. It is into this chamber we must now step.

5

The Aesthetic Dimension:
Only Words to Play With

ART AS DECEPTION

So far we have primarily discussed *Lolita* the way we might a realistic nineteenth-century novel by Balzac, George Eliot, or Mark Twain. We have mainly focused on the intricacies of psychology and characterization, on the reportorially rendered setting, and on such dominant humanistic concerns as the evils of child abuse and the dangers of solipsism, along the road touching on the work's fairly linear and clearly presented plot and chronology. In short, we have made certain assumptions about Nabokov's novel, key among them that we have been dealing with a text that aims to accurately render experience while taking a moral position toward its subject matter. Nabokov's sterling ability to paint his people as persuasively as he does has often convinced us that Humbert, Charlotte, and Dolly once really lived and spoke, acted and felt—so much so that we not infrequently find ourselves silently arguing with them, despising them or pitying them, rooting for them or condemning them, thinking of them as flesh-and-blood people with flesh-and-blood problems and flesh-and-blood desires.

We ought to take a moment now to remind ourselves that when contemplating those nineteenth-century novels, and especially when contemplating Nabokov's midtwentieth-century one, the impression of verisimilitude is just that: an impression. It is an illusion, a narrative slight of hand, a series of techniques and conventions designed by a gifted author to create the linguistic ghost of everyday life, the specters of fully-rounded characters and events, through an elaborate system of words that has at best an iffy connection with the plain facts and folks populating the world outside our window. Not that this realization should give us cause for disenchantment or frustration, cause to turn away from such texts as scant more than eggheaded games, complicated narrative betrayals of our ingenuous literary trust. Just the opposite. Understanding the deft craft and graceful magic that goes into generating such amazingly lifelike illusions should give us cause for greater enchantment and admiration, cause to appreciate them and their creators that much more. After all, simply because we know what the innards of a piano look like or how its strings, action, soundboard, and framework function in unison to yield beautiful music shouldn't cause us to enjoy the beautiful music they yield any less. Rather, such knowledge can—and should—add another dimension to our enjoyment.

Nabokov never lets the careful reader forget that he or she is watching a conjurer's show. Indeed, Nabokov regularly jogs our memories about such matters by giving us amorphous Clare Quilty, more malignant metaphor than realistic madman, or by short-circuiting his own moral sweep as author by infusing the novel with an energizing yet destabilizing comic impulse. The eminent lepidopterist thus continually calls our attention to the truth that *Lolita*, like his beloved butterflies in the wild, is a web of natural mimicry, an act of subterfuge, wherein what something is is nothing like what it seems to be. Keeping this in mind allows Nabokov's assertion that "art is deception and so is nature" to make sense (*SO*, 11). The author who loved to perform magic tricks as a child grew into the adult who loved to perform magic tricks in his writing, and it follows that for a consciousness like his "art at its greatest is fantastically deceitful and complex" (*SO*, 33)—not in any negative or mean-spiritedly fake way, but in the same liberating, dazzling, resourceful, talented, and very human way of the magician in the splendidly sequined suit who suddenly plucks a bountiful bouquet of spring flowers from thin air and holds them aloft for all to prize.

No doubt, of course, we as readers can conceptualize Nabokov's novel in moral terms. We have already done so at length. Yet also no doubt the aesthetic dimension of that novel always took precedence over the moral one in Nabokov's mind. Accordingly, when asked by a BBC interviewer in 1962 why he wrote his special favorite, Nabokov was quick to reply: "It was an interesting thing to do. Why did I write any of my books, after all? For the sake of the pleasure, for the sake of the difficulty. I have no social purpose, no moral message; I've no general ideas to exploit, I just like composing riddles with elegant solutions" (*SO*, 16). We are free to take exception with the author. We can assert that his fiction is in reality a deeply, humanistically moral achievement, that we should ultimately trust the tale and not the teller. But the author will continue to take exception with us by asserting that "a work of art has no importance whatever to society. . . . There can be no question that what makes a work of fiction safe from larvae and rust is not its social importance but its art, only its art" (*SO*, 33), or that "I have no purpose at all when composing my stuff except to compose it. I work hard. . . . If the reader has to work in his turn—so much the better. Art is difficult" (*SO*, 115). Even in his afterword to *Lolita*, he remained adamant about such matters: "I happen to be the kind of author who in starting to work on a book has no other purpose than to get rid of that book" (311); "it is childish to study a work of fiction in order to gain information about a country or about a social class or about the author" (316); "despite John Ray's assertion, *Lolita* has no moral in tow. For me a work of fiction exists only insofar as it affords me what I shall bluntly call aesthetic bliss" (314).

These sorts of persistent declarations link Nabokov to the aesthetic movement in Europe during the nineteenth century. Aesthetes such as Théophile Gautier, Oscar Wilde, and Aubrey Beardsley—influenced by Immanuel Kant's belief that aesthetic experience rested in a disinterested contemplation of the artwork at hand without reference to the universe beyond it or its moral ends, and by Edgar Allan Poe's belief that art was created for art's sake (hence the movement's French catchphrase, *l'art pour l'art*)—maintained that the reason art existed was for its formal perfection, its beauty, its elegance, its intricate artifice and stylistic subtlety, *not* for its utilitarian, moral, or social values. Perhaps this in small part accounts for the numerous references to artists and art in *Lolita*. Their presence drives this point home: that Nabokov's novel is one more exquisite creation among a constellation; it should be taken as no more (and no less) than that. Humbert surely holds nothing but contempt for such trendy, *poshlosty* modern art as "the cubistic trash" that Valeria paints (25), "that banal darling of the arty middle class, van Gogh's 'Arlésienne'" hanging in Charlotte's house (36), or "the obscene thing" Dolly shows him in a magazine depicting a Daliesque surrealist painter lying on a beach near a half-buried plastic replica of the Venus de Milo (58). But Hum cheers the stunning harmony of visual elements, the agile arrangement and precise representational craftsmanship, of "that tinge of Botticellian pink, that raw rose about [Dolly's] lips" (64). And he admires the "Claude-Lorrain clouds" and "stern El Greco horizon" that appear above the couple on their cross-country sojourn (152), and even the plates of works by Grant Wood and Peter Hurd from the *History of Modern American Painting* that he innocently buys for the comic-book-loving Dolly for her birthday (199). Nabokov seems to concur extratextually by remarking that what made Picasso great was "the graphic aspect, the masterly technique, and the quiet colors. But then, starting with *Guernica*, his production leaves me indifferent. The aspects of Picasso that I emphatically dislike are the sloppy products of his old age." His favorites? "Mostly Russian and French painters. And English artists such as Turner" (*SO*, 166–67).

Nabokov found particular pleasure in trompe l'oeil paintings, those by creators such as Renaissance artist Mantegna and nineteenth-century artist William Michael Harnett, which attempt to deceive the viewer's eye as to the material reality of the objects they represent: that nail apparently sticking out of the frame, which turns out to have been painted on; that postage stamp seemingly stuck in a corner; that playing card presumably tucked along an edge. "A good *trompe l'oeil* painting proves at least that the painter is not cheating," Nabokov declared. "The charlatan who sells his squiggles to *épatér* Philistines does not have the talent or the technique to draw a nail, let alone the shadow of a nail" (*SO*, 167). Talent and technique: these in many ways are the hallmarks of *Lolita*, a novel that often partakes of a fictional variety of trompe l'oeil, playing games of perception with multiple levels of reality and interpretation, rendering its world in such a seemingly naturalistic manner that the reader is "tricked" into thinking it is actually three-dimensional, always proving that the novelist isn't cheating, that he can draw a nail as well as its shadow, finely highlighting Humbert as well as Clare the Impredictable.

Hence theorist Harold Bloom's pronouncement that *Lolita* is "baroque and subtle," "a book written to be reread."[1] And hence Nabokov's snide rebuttal to the accusation by his critics that his writing is too obscure, too meticulously elite, too knottily difficult and numbingly involved to digest easily. Such readers, he said, should "stick to the crossword puzzle in their Sunday paper" (*SO*, 184). His baroque narrative is composed not for them but for the thorough reader who understands that art is difficult and that in its difficulty lies its pleasure. It is for the kind of person who notes in passing in chapter 11 that Dolly's favorite record is "Little Carmen," and who thereby remembers not Georges Bizet's popular 1875 opera but Prosper Mérimée's less celebrated 1845 novella, in which the protagonist, Don José, murders his lover, the clever young gypsy Carmen, out of a sense of revenge and rage when she claims their passionate affair is over. And for the kind of person who then files away each instance where Humbert quotes Mérimée (243, 278, 280) and each where he calls Dolly "Carmen" (59, 60, 61, 242–43, 251, 256, 278, 280), assuming all the while, given this evidence, that Humbert will finally kill *his* unfaithful lover. But then Nabokov pulls the whole complicated Persian rug out from under the reader, when Dolly for one last time turns down Hum's request that she come live with him, and he announces: "Then I pulled out my automatic—I mean, this is the kind of fool thing a reader might suppose I did. It never even occurred to me to do it" (280).

Voilà: trompe l'oeil fiction, mischievous fiction that creates a richly textured, "realistic" universe only to remind us through its subtle sorcery that that universe isn't realistic at all. *The Enchanted Hunters*, the playlet-within-the-book in which Dolly acts, becomes a microcosm for the sum: it exists (as did such plays-within-plays in Elizabethan drama and in the work of such modern and postmodern outriders of the tradition as Luigi Pirandello and Tom Stoppard) to underscore the fact that we the viewers/readers are experiencing talented and technical art, not life, and that our knowledge of the text and world stands on nothing if not shaky ground. So the Borgesian seventh hunter in Dolly's drama is none other than the Young Poet, an artist figure (who nonetheless wears a fool's cap), who insists that Dolly and the others in the piece aren't real at all, but "his, the Poet's, invention" (201). Obviously, this observation is true at the level of the playlet. But it is also true at the level of *Lolita* itself, and in a number of ways: Dolly's character in the play is Quilty's invention; Dolly's character in the confession we're reading is Humbert's; and all the characters in the novel are Nabokov's. To a certain extent, then, *Lolita* exists in order to tease us, to dangle the interpretive carrot in front of us only to jerk it away again and again. To a certain extent, however, it also exists in order to reward our energy in reading, to compliment our diligence in interpretation, and, in the end, to provide us with a bounty of opulent intellectual and emotional enjoyments.

THE LITERATURE OF ALLUSION

Another portal into that palace of intellectual delights is the discovery of some of the more important literary allusions in Nabokov's narrative. As Alfred Appel, Jr., makes clear in his instructive introduction to the annotated version of the book, *Lolita* is no less than the "most allusive . . . novel in English since *Ulysses* and *Finnegans Wake*" (ix). Nabokov refers to more than 60 writers in the novel, usually from English and French literature, frequently to the very poets, novelists, and dramatists he himself translated during his émigré years in Germany (Baudelaire, Byron, Carroll, Goethe, Keats, Pushkin, Rimbaud, Ronsard, Shakespeare, and Verlaine among them). His

intent was not simply to wow the well-read with his literary sophistication but to create complex juxtapositions between the original subject and the allusion to it, ironic dismantlings, serious tributes, multiple
perspectives, playful parodies, and interesting expansions with which
to view *Lolita*'s characters, plot, setting, and themes. While in much
early literature (we might think of works by Sophocles, Milton, and
Pope, for instance) the author could assume that explicit or indirect
allusions to people, events, or other texts would be caught and fath-
omed by the contemporary educated reader, in much modern and
postmodern literature (we might think of works by Joyce, Eliot, and
Pynchon) the author regularly employs specialized or exceedingly private allusions with the understanding that few readers will recognize
them without the aid of scholarly annotation. Certainly we can number Nabokov among these latter writers.

Prominent among his literary references are ones to such suitably
breathtaking stylists as Shakespeare, Flaubert, and Joyce. Nabokov
hints at *Hamlet* at least twice, for instance, *Macbeth* once. We learn in
Who's Who in the Limelight that an actor named Roland Pym (his
name, by the way, an allusion to Poe's *The Narrative of Arthur Gordon
Pym*) trained at *Elsinore* Playhouse in Derby, New York (31). Quoting
from a book on how to raise young girls about the way one's father
figure is "forerunner of the desired elusive male," Humbert inserts parenthetically, "'elusive' is good, by Polonius!" thereby summoning up
the gabby elder in Shakespeare's 1602 drama, and quite possibly his
caveats to his devoted if doomed daughter, Ophelia, about menacing
men (150). These nods to *Hamlet* serve Nabokov's more general aims
of highlighting key themes and leitmotifs like revenge, ghosts, the
play-within-the-play, father-daughter relationships, questions of
morality and selfhood, madness, jealousy, and artifice. In addition to
these winks at the Bard, there is Quilty's poor pun on Macbeth's
somber soliloquy, a literary gesture underpinning the themes of retri-
bution and universal McFatedness (301). Flaubert surfaces both in the
form of his well-known aesthetic dictum, *le mot juste* ("the right
word" [47], his advice to writers everywhere about the importance of
craft and grace in composition), and in the form of a reference (just
below one to another of Shakespeare's plays, *King Lear*) to part 3,

chapter 8, of his most famous novel, a scandalous success in its own day, *Madame Bovary*. The heroine's husband, a pharmacist, and a physician attempt to save Emma Bovary's life after she suicidally ingests poison; as Nabokov writes, no matter how many times we open Flaubert's text, "never will Emma rally" (265). The import of this allusion is to remind us of how the real has undone the ideal in Emma's as well as Dolly-Humbert's world and of how in both works every literary character's "fate is fixed" (265). Joyce, whose *Ulysses* Nabokov taught in his European fiction course at Cornell and greatly admired for its "noble originality and unique lucidity" (*SO*, 71), appears on two significant occasions in the novel. First he is acknowledged in Nabokov's subtle French grin of appreciation (*"J'ai toujours admiré l'oeuvre ormonde du sublime Dublinois,"* or "I have always admired the [ormonde] work of the sublime Dubliner" [207]), brought up ironically as Dolly watches a waitress concoct a cherry coke in a nearby drugstore, with reference to Dublin's Hotel Ormond, whose restaurant figures in the "Sirens" episode of *Ulysses*. Second, Joyce emerges in Nabokov's appreciative multilingual parody of stream-of-consciousness as Dolly climbs into Humbert's arms at the Enchanted Hunters (*"Elevator clatterans, pausa, clatterans, populus in corridoro . . ."* etc. [120]).

An additional group of artists to whom Nabokov alludes are the fin-de-siècle decadents, a subset of the aesthetes who believed that late nineteenth-century European civilization, like the late Roman Empire, had passed its prime and fallen into delicious decay. Resolutely opposed to biological and social "nature," these creators cultivated baroque styles and bizarre subject matter, often experimenting with drugs and sexual extremes. Humbert Humbert, kindred spirit to such authors as Oscar Wilde in England and Joris Karl Huysmans in France, embodies a Byzantine sense of artifice, a passion for an illicit substance (in his case alcohol), a deep devotion to socially unacceptable forms of sexuality, and an arch existential sense of lassitude and ennui. Like several of the decadents, he also dies young, in his early 40s. So it comes as small surprise that the word *Beardsley*, echo of decadent artist Aubrey Beardsley, as we have already seen, plays such a resonant role in the novel. It is applied to the town and college where Humbert and

Dolly live for a spell, and it is associated with Gaston Godin (a painter of sorts), whose grotesque portrait Beardsley might happily have painted and whose house Huysmans would have admired, with its orientally furnished den and studio lined with photographs of such famous gay creators as André Gide, Tchaikovsky, and Marcel Proust. It is equally remarkable that Charles Baudelaire, whose poems in *Les Fleurs du Mal* are prefaced by what amounts to a manifesto of decadence by Théophile Gautier, makes several appearances in the narrative (162, 262, 284).

No confession claiming the status of a great love story would be complete without numerous allusions to famous literary lovers as well. We have already mentioned Nabokov's revealing use of Roman poet Catullus and his love for Lesbia (66), Dante and his for Beatrice (19), Petrarch and his for Laura (19), and Poe and his for Annabel (9, 12, 13, 31, 39, etc.). To these we can add an allusion to Jonathan Swift, who educated and came to love Esther Johnson, the young daughter of a steward ("Stella" in his writing), and who awakened a violent passion in a much younger woman, Hester Vanhomrigh (his "Vanessa") (12). Lewis Carroll apparently sends over "a breeze from wonderland" to disturb Humbert's mind at the Enchanted Hunters (131), and there is a later reference to "a half-naked nymphet stilled in the act of combing her Alice-in-Wonderland hair" (264). Nabokov, devoted enough to Carroll's work to translate *Alice in Wonderland* into Russian in 1923 for the equivalent of $5, felt the Oxford mathematician had "a pathetic affinity with H. H. but some odd scruple prevented me from alluding in *Lolita* to his perversion and to those ambiguous photographs he took in dim rooms. . . . [of] sad scrawny little nymphets, bedraggled and half-undressed, or rather semi-undraped, as if participating in some dusty and dreadful charade." Something prevented him from *directly* alluding to the "perversion," but there are more than enough *indirect* allusions, especially in the guise of Humbert's fascination with photographs of young girls and in the fact that Hum (as Nabokov says of Carroll) "got away with it, as so many other Victorians got away with pederasty and nympholepsy" (*SO*, 81).[2]

It is a short step from Humbert's misuse of Dante and Beatrice's love, or his deft suggestion of Carroll's fetish, to another cluster of literary references—those to stories like Nabokov's involving psychologically unhinged protagonists and/or narrators. Among these we can include the Marquis de Sade's *Justine, or The Misfortunes of Virtue*, which, not unlike *Lolita*, is prefaced by a highly moral foreword and concerns the story of a brave, young (12 when her narrative begins, we are told) girl's trials and tribulations at the hands of a string of sadists (276). Fittingly, Quilty has made "private movies out of *Justine* and other eighteenth-century sexcapades" (298). Nabokov also waves a number of times to Robert Browning, conjuring up on the reader's part recollections of the nineteenth-century poet's celebratedly unstable and unreliable narrators in such poems as "Porphyria's Lover" and "Childe Roland to the Dark Tower Came." And he shows appreciation for Browning's verse technique of the dramatic monologue, which Humbert's confession suggests. Both Nabokov and Browning employ a single person speaking in a single situation at an important moment, addressing at least one other person and unintentionally revealing his character through what he says and how he says it (117, 207, 242, 245). Robert Louis Stevenson's presence in the text triggers memories of his classic tale of the doppelgänger, *Dr. Jekyll and Mr. Hyde*, with its multilingual pun in the title (*je* and *kyll*) hinting at the self-murder the unbalanced Humbert must commit in order to integrate his personality (158, 206).

A final powerful literary presence in *Lolita* is Marcel Proust's monumental opus, *Remembrance of Things Past*. An early essay Humbert writes is on "the Proustian theme" in a letter by Keats (16). He refers to his confession as a series of "Proustian intonations" (77). And Proust himself is named or alluded to on at least three other occasions in the course of the narrative (182, 253, 264). Each of these citations reminds us of the French author's cardinal themes, time and memory, both so precious to Humbert and Nabokov. For all three writers, everything in the world is bound by time on the one hand and freed from time on the other by associational memory. A simple taste of madeleine soaked in a decoction of lime-flowers launches adult Marcel into volumes of recollection about his youth, while the whole of *Lolita* is no less than an associational narrative about the past that attempts to revisit and freeze physically lost moments through art into eternal memorial shrines. Memory, then, in a sense allows us to move beyond clock-time, an idea that takes us back to the point made earlier about Humbert's romantic attempt to transcend mere *chronos*, that realm of chronology always ticking toward death, and reach a state of poetic *kairos*, that divine and intensely subjective realm of timelessness associated with love and art.

THE GENETICS OF GENRE

Genre denotes a type or species of literature. Each type or species exhibits a specific series of conventions and codes that form a kind of contract between writer and reader about what the former will deliver and the latter expect. This seems simple and straightforward enough. If we come across a brief concentrated utterance told from a first-person point of view, chances are we are dealing with lyric. If we read a text apparently designed to amuse us in which the action tends to turn out happily for the protagonists, chances are we are in the compass of comedy. But what happens when a literary work deliberately uses and abuses traditional genres, deliberately violates that contract between writer and reader? What happens when the clear, clean lines separating one genre from another begin to break down?

What often happens is the creation of a startlingly new and intriguing work, a literary mutant frequently dubbed an experimental or anti-novel, which captures our imagination, challenges our ability to crack its conventions and codes, and jogs us alert again to questions concerning traditional narrative norms. What happens, in short, is a text like *Lolita*, which enfolds and extends a literary lineage that includes such grand radical investigations as Laurence Sterne's *Tristram Shandy*, William Faulkner's *The Sound and the Fury*, and Samuel Beckett's *Molloy*, showing us both the limitations and the possibilities inherent in a particular form. A book like *Lolita* hence at least in part achieves its greatness through its ability to surprise us by rewriting the contract between writer and reader. Or, as Nabokov put it:

"Every original novel is 'anti-' because it does not resemble the genre or kind of its predecessor" (*SO*, 173).

It follows, to summon up the influential ideas of Russian theorist Mikhail Bakhtin, that "genre is always the same and not the same, always old and new simultaneously. A genre is reborn and renewed at every stage in the development of literature and in every individual work of the given genre. This gives the genre life."[3] Just as the convention of allusion directly or indirectly refers to people, events, or other texts to make its point while revitalizing our perceptions of both the original text and the allusive one, so too the convention of genre can be used by experimental writers (and we should remember here that all writers, save for the most generic, are experimental) to refer directly or indirectly to previous manipulations of genre to make its point while revitalizing our perceptions of both the general genre and the specific instance of it. Genre in an experimental text therefore becomes a subspecies of allusion. And *Lolita* is a veritable Mulligan stew of allusive genres. It shape-shifts as it proceeds, calling forth a wealth of fictional forms, sometimes for the brief space of a sentence or three, sometimes for chapters on end. The intent behind this is multiple. Such a narrative gesture concentrates the reader's attention on the novel's processes, displays Nabokov's knowledge of literary history, shakes our beliefs about genre and writing itself, and generates illuminating if frequently ironic juxtapositions between traditional genres and Nabokov's use of them, playful plaudits and parodies, invigorating expansions and explorations—all with an aim to amplify the deep structural instability of the text itself.

Many readers, triggered by the revelation of the book's full title in the first line of foreword by John Ray, Jr., conceptualize *Lolita* as a confession, a form of autobiography with antecedents in works by such writers as Saint Augustine, Jean-Jacques Rousseau, and Thomas De Quincey. Confession customarily probes highly confidential and highly personal matters while maintaining an introspective intellectual emphasis. Related to this is another autobiographical form, the memoir, which usually focuses less on the intellectual and private life of its subject than on its subject's recollections of significant personalities and events. *Lolita* partakes of conventions from both, but the intriguing question to ask is why. One reply is that by shaping a confessional memoir through the eyes of a thoroughly unreliable and deeply disturbed narrator, Nabokov problematizes the very notion of autobiography, the capacity to honestly and accurately record one's life in words. At the same time, he reminds us of the fictional dimension to all history—including the local history of the self. Although it is true enough, as Proust maintained, that time and memory play essential roles in human consciousness, it is equally true that memory can amount to little more than a fabrication of time in the hands of flawed Humbert with his flawed mind. And therefore, Nabokov seems to ask, what about the rest of us? To answer that question, we must enter the realm of epistemology. What can we know about ourselves and our history for certain, and how? What is the difference between believing we know something, wanting to know something, pretending to know something, and actually knowing it?

But *Lolita* is much more than a confessional memoir. It is, as John Ray, Jr., alerts us, a psychiatric case study of a pedophile, a pathological liar, and a murderer. In short, it is part of a genre that was for all intents and purposes invented by Freud—and yet, ironically, it is a novel filled with anti-Freudian sentiment. With one arm Nabokov embraces the father of psychoanalysis, with the other pushes him away, and the outcome, as we have already witnessed, is an extremely complex relationship between the two. We have noted besides how *Lolita* is an example of the tale of the mysterious doppelgänger, or double, in the tradition of Poe's "William Wilson." Yet it also touches on the forms of diary, legal defense, and travel journal (particularly the mid-century incarnation of the Michelin guidebook). It is a romantic novel in the tradition of Victor Hugo's *The Hunchback of Notre Dame* and Poe's *The Narrative of Arthur Gordon Pym*, with its dark undercurrents of Gothic horror, its solitary protagonist, and its infinitely elusive quest. Yet it also shares much with the realistic novel in the tradition of Flaubert's *Madame Bovary* and Twain's *The Adventures of Huckleberry Finn*, with its commitment to local detail, accurately rendered time and place, and exploration of middle-class reality.

It is at once a comedy, with its use of verbal cartwheels, wit, acidic irony, situational slapstick, burlesque, parody, satire, and so on, and a tragedy, with its serious import, its Aristotelian arousal of pity and fear in the reader, its protagonist's *hamartia*, or error in judgment, with respect to his relationship with Dolly, its revenge motif, its disastrous ending for Humbert and his victim, and even the narrator's and our possible spiritual catharsis or purgation during its final pages in Pavor Manor. In equal parts it also exemplifies and parodies the traditional love story, in which the protagonists overcome various hardships to be united forever; medieval romance, with its hunt structures, its themes of jealousy and repeated attempts to surmount sexual obstacles to attain its goal; the mythic quest, be it Jason's for the Golden Fleece or the German romantics's struggle to *streben nach dem Unendlichen*, or strive for the infinite; the picaresque narrative, with its episodic structure, satiric intent, focus on the escapades of a rascal who lives by his wits, and, in the case of one of the most splendid examples of the genre, *Don Quixote*, its exploration of a madman's confusion of illusion and reality.

Lolita even has many affinities with the fairy tale in its pervasive sense of magic and its story line about a man who slips under the perilous spell of a sprite who subjects him to a series of mischievous pranks and adventures. The novel is rife with references to Lewis Carroll, *Hansel and Gretel*, and *Bluebeard*. Dolly is "a fairy princess" (52) who plays "beauty" to Humbert's "beast" (59). Humbert in turn masquerades as "Prince Charming" (109). The pills Dolly takes at "the pale palace" (117) of the Enchanted Hunters are referred to both as a "magic potion" and as "Beauty's Sleep" (122). The word Elphinstone becomes catalyst for various fairy-tale puns. Hum significantly presents Dolly on her birthday with a deluxe edition of Hans Christian Andersen's *The Little Mermaid*, a story about a diminutive being who enchants a human heart, while on several occasions Hum refers to himself as a merman (86, 255). The supernatural numbers 3 and 1001 drift through the text, and hunters, nymphs, elves, and monsters through the fairy-tale play in which Dolly acts. Mentions of enchanted keys and dwellings, castles and dungeons, demons and flying carpets proliferate, and Hum's story culminates in none other than the eerie rooms of Pavor Manor situated on none other than Grimm Road (the latter a spoofy bow toward the German brothers Jacob and Wilhelm, who pioneered the study of folklore and fairy tales in the nineteenth century). That manor's door swings open "as in a medieval fairy tale" (294) upon a darkly fantastic universe.

The purpose of this massive participation in the fairy-tale genre is icily ironic. In the apparent antimatter of a fairy-tale abode, Dick and Dolly's tottery house, white-knight Hum pleads with his aged, towered damsel to accompany him to his car and escape with him into contentment. "Make those twenty five steps," he tells her. "Now. Right now. Come just as you are. And we shall live happily ever after" (278). But that is the one thing McFate has not planned for them. In Nabokov's pages, the wretched real of the world wrecks the fairy-tale idealization every time.

A final important genre in which *Lolita* is involved is the detective story. This is especially obvious during the cryptogrammic paper chase when we find ourselves entering an extended parody of the Poeian tale of ratiocination. The essence of that tale concerns an astute sleuth's attempts to solve a mystery by logically assembling and interpreting evidence. The problem in this particular example of the tale is that it isn't at all clear whether hallucinating Humbert is reading real clues or whether those "clues" are, like the multitude of detectives he believes hot on his trail, "figments of [his] persecution mania, recurrent images based on coincidence and chance resemblance" (238). As if to drive home this genre's presence, Nabokov seeds his text with variations of Poe's name, from Harry Edgar (43) to Dr. Edgar H. Humbert (118), while alluding to the originator of the detective story no fewer than 23 other times. Meanwhile, Arthur Conan Doyle's Sherlock Holmes feminizes into Shirley Holmes (64); Agatha Christie's novel *A Murder Is Announced* is announced one page before Quilty's murder is signaled via the title of a play called *The Murdered Playwright* (32); and one of Christie's nineteenth-century French counterparts, Maurice Leblanc, is referred to at least twice (211, 250).

A staple of the detective story, the red herring or false clue, surfaces a number of times as well—by means, for instance, of those frequent references to Carmen that lead us to imagine Humbert will kill

Dolly (45, 59, 62, 209); or the letter that Humbert receives just as Dolly leaves for camp and that appears to have been written by her, but turns out to be from Charlotte (67–68); or Dolly's desire to climb a mountain where a screen star leaped to her death after "a drunken row with her gigolo," a wish that leads us to suspect Dolly might commit suicide after her affair with Quilty (210). Aligned with these red herrings are authentic clues so mischievously minuscule as to be completely overlooked during our first, second, or even third readings: by way of illustration, the big pink bubble that forms on the dying Quilty's lips (304) is first blown in chapter 5 (17); and Quilty's "Ah," his cry of surprise and anguish as Humbert shoots him repeatedly at the end of the novel (303), is first uttered by a polar bear that in chapter 11 Humbert recounts shooting on his arctic visit (45).

With these lilliputian tips we find ourselves once more peering over the shoulder of the entomologist who counted the scale-rows of a butterfly's wing markings under a microscope for fun. Nabokov's abiding love of the precise thereby remanifests itself, and we are reminded of his observation that "only myopia condones the blurry generalizations of ignorance. In high art and pure science detail is everything" (SO, 168). Another level is accordingly added to our discussion of his use of the detective story. Not only is the poor protagonist an obsessive if bumbling sleuth who must sort and shift, decipher and deduce the clues swarming through his narrative universe, but so too must Nabokov's ideal reader be an obsessive if bumbling sleuth who must attempt to decode the author's teasing textual games. If we do not spend the time and energy necessary to crack his puzzles, if we do not finally agree with Humbert that "there is always delight in the semi-translucent mystery" (53), then we have missed the author's point.

This is never clearer than on three pivotal occasions in the novel. First is when we come across Hum's transcription of most of that page from *Who's Who in the Limelight* (31). Here, as we have already found, our job is to take note of such enticing information as the fact that Clare Quilty is author of plays appropriately entitled *The Little Nymph*, *Dark Age*, and *Fatherly Love*, all carrying references to his pedophilia, as well as *The Lady Who Loved Lightning*, with its astounding acknowledgment of Humbert's mother's bizarre death ("astounding" because it stands to reason that Quilty knows nothing of the event—unless, that is, he is a figment of Humbert's imagination, or unless Nabokov is nudging our memory about the fact that Quilty is a figment of his). Or that the name of Cue's collaborator, Vivian Darkbloom, is an anagram for Vladimir Nabokov. Or that Cue's hobbies (fast cars, photography, and pets) are all previsions of his perverse affair with Dolly and stay at Duk Duk Ranch.

Second is when we come across Dolly's class roster, discovered by Humbert in a volume of the *Young Person's Encyclopedia* (51–52). Here our mission is to remark such interesting specifics as the fact that the list is mimeographed on the back of a map of the United States, a situation that both foreshadows Dolly and Hum's cross-country journeys and accentuates the dimensions of the chessboard on which the two play out their relationship. Or that the reference to Jack and Mary Beale previews Charlotte's death, since it is the Beales's father who runs her over. Or that in the puckish catalog there are no fewer than four sets of twinned names, suggesting the novel's double theme. Or that McFate himself makes a cameo. Or that Quilty's color red and Dolly's rose permeate the names. Or that Ted Falter's last name is German for, what else, butterfly.

Third is when we embark with Humbert on that famous cryptogrammic paper chase in which the world itself becomes a dizzyingly rich, provocative, and potentially threatening text (250–52). Here the fields of data are too large to sift through quickly or thoroughly at one reading, but we should again be aware of and take pleasure in the small: in the fact that, for instance, Coleridge is summoned up by the mention of "A. Person, Porlock, England," since it was the person from Porlock who allegedly interrupted the poet's composition of "Kubla Khan"; and Molière by the mention of "D. Orgon, Elmira, NY," since Orgon is Elmire's husband in *Tartuffe*, a play about, among other things, seduction and the distance between the seeming and the real. Or that Arthur Rimbaud ("Rainbow"), Aristophanes ("N. S. Aristoff"), Aubrey Beardsley, Donald Quix(ote), Carmen, Shakespeare (his years, like Cue's license numbers, run from "WS 1564" to "SH

1616"), and even the deceased Harold Haze (of, no less, "Tombstone, Arizona") also make brief appearances. Or that, reinforcing the sexual overtones running throughout the book, "Dr. Kitzler, Eryx, Miss." suggests both the German for clitoris (*Kitzler*) and the ancient cult of Aphrodite of Eryx, goddess of love and beauty, while "Will Brown, Dolores, Colo.," suggests the sodomy Quilty performs on Dolly. Or that, if we bring out our pencil for some fast math, we learn the last two mirrory license plate numbers cited ("Q32888" and "CU 88322") add up to 52, the number of weeks Hum and Dolly remain on the road between August 1947 and August 1948.

If Nabokov inverts and thus subverts the fairy-tale genre by ultimately showing us that no one lives happily ever after, he then inverts and thus subverts the detective genre by giving us the end long before the beginning. He names the murderer up front, putting us in the unconventional position of having to figure out through the course of the novel who the murderer murdered rather than who the murdered was murdered by, and he informs us through John Ray, Jr., that all the main characters in the text are already dead long before we begin reading, putting us in the unconventional position of having to figure out through the course of the novel not the mystery surrounding their demises but the mystery surrounding their lives. Moreover, by such funning with the detective genre, Nabokov brings us face to face with further serious epistemological questions.

As with his use of the confessional memoir, here we find ourselves asking what can be known with certainty about ourselves, our perceptions, and our world, and we find ourselves discovering uncomfortably that the answer is very little indeed. The universe, Nabokov intimates, may prove to be a splendid, densely woven puzzle ultimately able to be deciphered through meticulously extended enterprise. But if the truth is that we are all versions of Humbert Humbert, all human beings with defective perception and defective souls, then it may also only appear to our obsessive, almost paranoid eyes to offer the promise of elegant solutions, when in fact all it gives back is our desperate need to make breathtaking and life-affirming connections where none actually exist.

THE METAPHOR OF METAMORPHOSIS

Lolita's elision of genres leads us to the doorstep of the dominant metaphor at work within the text: metamorphosis. Although most young mammals such as hamsters and horses differ in size rather than form and structure from their parents, the young of such insects as Nabokov's cherished butterfly look radically different from mature specimens. Startling changes take place as the butterfly develops from an embryo inside its egg into the larva, its newly hatched caterpillar or wormlike stage; through the pupa, where the larva encloses itself in a chrysalis; to the imago, or adult stage, where the fully developed butterfly finally emerges from its chrysalis after a period of 10 to 14 days. Biologists refer to these abrupt alterations in form and structure as metamorphoses, and we have seen analogous sudden transformations occur at the level of genre in Nabokov's novel. But they take place at other levels as well. The text itself, for instance, develops from sketchy notes jotted by Humbert in jail as he awaits trial into a full-fledged manuscript in the hands of his editor, John Ray, Jr. And that manuscript itself continually transmutes from realistic account to self-conscious game as we read it.

Characters, too, undergo various kinds of metamorphosis. Charlotte transmutes from a living being into a dead one. Quilty, an emblem of the text as a whole, is described as "a veritable Proteus" (227), an epithet linking him to the sea god of Greek mythology who could quickly change shapes when caught in order to elude his captors. Humbert, whose academic projects involve translation, or linguistic metamorphosis, and whose name undergoes a wide variety of transfigurations during his confession, watches as his sexual desire transforms into humane love, his impulse to make Dolly his own into one that grants her genuine, generous freewill, and his struggle with his dark half into his capacity to shed the Quilty within and possibly gain something approaching a steady moral center. His sordid transgressions even modulate into a gracefully rendered piece of enduring art. The object of his affections, whose name alters from Dolly Haze to Dolores to Lo to Lola to Lolita to Dolly Schiller, is an innocent nymphet (a word suggesting, among other things, that insect in the pupal stage of metamorphosis) who develops into a mature, savvy adult who in turn spreads her wings to fly away from Humbert and the restrictive existence he has attempted to create for her. In each of these instances, there is an underlying emphasis on the instability of selfhood, the ability of the self to mutate quickly, thoroughly, and repeatedly through one's life.

Even at the level of language itself, metamorphosis is present. Under Humbert's gaze, words mutate into multilingual puns, anagrams, and double entendres. Key names like the "Enchanted Hunters," suggesting Hum and Cue's pursuit of Dolly, as well as the fairy-tale theme, undergo continual variation, beginning in chapter 5, when Humbert remembers sharing with Annabel an "enchanted island of time" (18). The name resurfaces as the hotel where Hum and Dolly spend their first night together (108); as the name of Quilty's play (200); as—according to Miss Pratt's appropriate mishearing of the play's title—*The Hunted Enchanters* (196); as Cue's clever anagram "Ted Hunter, Cane, NH" during the cryptogrammic paper chase (251); and, finally, as Dick and Dolly's Hunter Road (268), devoid of enchantment altogether. More subtly, Nabokov takes a single, seemingly incidental word or phrase and toys with it through the course of the entire novel. "Chestnut mare," to cite one example, first appears in chapter 20 as part of a caustic metaphor for Jean Farlow's uninteresting legs (80). Thirty-seven pages later the color returns at the Enchanted Hunters in the sentence, "Under the arclights enlarged replicas of chestnut leaves plunged and played on white pillars" (117). Almost 100 pages later we find a tepid rain falling on similar "chestnut leaves" (206), and then, in fairly rapid succession, those leaves reform into "Chestnut Court" (212), "chestnut trees" (212), "Chestnut Castle" (213), "Chestnut Crest" (213), again "Chestnut Court" (215), and then, through a sprinkle of magic, from trees and motels into horses in the phrase "the reader must now forget Chestnuts and Colts" (216). But if we heed Hum's advice, and do indeed forget them, we shall miss the smell of "chestnuts and roses" 25 pages down the line (241), not to mention the whole town of Chestnut mentioned 7 pages after that.

The Aesthetic Dimension: Only Words to Play With

The consequence of such relentless metamorphic playfulness is to remind us once more that at the register of technique Nabokov is supreme monarch of his domain. Bereft of his Lolita, Hum hopelessly declares: "I have only words to play with!" (32). Yet he and Nabokov play with them masterfully. At the same time, their very act of play underscores the instability of language itself. Nabokov's sporting with a name like the "Enchanted Hunters" or a word like "chestnut" calls to mind Jacques Derrida's deconstructionist notion of *différance*, itself a pun whose spelling conflates two senses of the French word *différence*: that of "difference" and that of "deferment." For Derrida, as for Ferdinand de Saussure, the Swiss structuralist against whose ideas Derrida often defines himself, the meaning of a word is created by its differences from innumerable other meanings and words. So in English *cat* means *cat* only because it doesn't mean *bat* or *hat*. But since the meaning of a word is defined only by its difference from other meanings and words, and not by any inherently stable or essential meaning within it, it can never possess absolute presence. Thus its exact meaning will always be deferred from one interpretative situation to another. The result is a series of transformations without end, and the implication that language is a continual play of difference and deferment, of *différance*, where determinate meaning is infinitely elusive, infinitely (to echo Quilty's personality) protean.

Nabokov's metamorphic playfulness serves as well to remind us just how unstable the bedrock of our existence is. Not only language but also selfhood, time, place, and condition are wont to change abruptly, like the butterfly larva into the imago, without warning and for little apparent reason. For Nabokov himself life was a succession of seismic shock waves, jolting him from financial security to poverty, from political poise to revolution, from world peace to world war, from the elegance of late nineteenth-century St. Petersburg to the relative squalor of early twentieth-century European émigré communities, from writing in one language to writing in another, from virtual anonymity to overnight global success, and from his motherland in Russia to exile in Europe, then America, and then back to Europe again. It is therefore little wonder that a sense of perpetual and sudden conversion, uncertainty, dislocation, and precipitous surprise should suffuse his narrative universe so thoroughly. Metamorphosis wasn't simply a metaphor for him. It was a way of being in the world.

TALKING LIKE A BOOK

A closer look at one of those subsets of metamorphosis: Nabokov's continual impulse to shape-shift *Lolita* from an ostensibly realistic novel into one that keeps calling attention to itself *as* a novel. On their ride from Camp Q to the Enchanted Hunters, Hum and Dolly swerve into a sexually charged conversation:

> We rolled silently through a silent townlet.
> "Say, wouldn't Mother be absolutely mad if she found out we were lovers?" [asks Dolly.]
> "Good Lord, Lo, let us not talk that way."
> "But we *are* lovers, aren't we?"
> "Not that I know of. I think we are going to have some more rain. Don't you want to tell me of those little pranks of yours in camp?"
> "You talk like a book, *Dad*."
> "What have you been up to? I insist you tell me." (114)

As the scene begins to drift ominously toward a serious revelation about the nature of Hum and Dolly's relationship, Hum changes the subject by pointing to possible rain and raising questions about Dolly's stay at camp. Nabokov also changes the subject by having Dolly, suddenly his narrative puppet, announce that both Hum and she are living in a novel. Humbert Humbert does indeed talk like a book. And he *should*, all said and done, since he's living in one. The text, only a blink of an eye before enacting the conventions of a traditional novel of character and conflict, without warning takes a quantum leap into self-reflexivity, and then back again into the conventions of a traditional novel of character and conflict, with Hum's demand to know what Dolly's been up to. Nabokov thereby winks at the reader through his curtain of prose. Doing so, he accomplishes several objectives. He shows himself to be keenly aware that he is composing a work of fiction. He reminds us that realism isn't real. And he flaunts the immense incongruities between the artifice he is constructing and the reality it apparently tries to mirror.

With this kind of self-conscious mischief rollicking at the text's core, we might expect to find sports, both intellectual and physical, playing an important role in *Lolita* as emblems of the larger textual games that Nabokov executes. And we wouldn't be let down. Chess, with its accent on logic, grace, and cunning, as well as its focus on its queen and its central metaphor of conflict, dominates the novel. Humbert first enters a round with Valeria's father, then queenly Gaston Godin in bi- and triweekly failures. America, too, becomes a massive gameboard on which Hum and Cue battle for possession of Dolly. Tennis plays a significant metaphoric role in the book as well. It is, after all, an old gray tennis ball lying on an oak chest that initially signals Dolly's presence in Charlotte's house (39), and it is Dolly's tennis game that produces an "indescribable itch of rapture" in Humbert, a "teasing delirious feeling of teetering on the very brink of unearthly order and splendor" (230). Although her game is weak, Dolly's form is flawless, and watching that "vital web of balance between toed foot, pristine armpit, burnished arm and far back-flung racket, as she smiled up with gleaming teeth at the small globe suspended so high in the zenith of the powerful and graceful cosmos" brings Humbert as close to an exquisite Keatsian moment of *kairos* as he is ever likely reach (231). Both chess and tennis also function as fine metaphors for Hum and Dolly's sparring partnership, even for their lopsided love and/or "marriage," embodied in both sports's perpetual give and take, primary adversarial relationship, and calculating mode of competition that sets one opponent's intellectual or physical skill against another's. We are reminded of the second section of Eliot's *The Waste Land*, in which relationships between the sexes are shown to be little more, as the title of that section indicates, than games of chess. Mentions of other sports—including kissing (just an amusing diversion for Dolly), horseshoes, butterfly collecting, jump rope, cards, puzzles, baseball, and swimming—only accentuate these tendencies.

"The verbal poetical texture of Shakespeare is the greatest the world has known, and is immensely superior to the structure of his plays as plays," Nabokov told Alfred Appel, Jr., in 1966. "With Shakespeare it is the metaphor that is the thing, and not the play" (*SO*, 90). In Nabokov's case, it is frequently the language that is the thing, and not the novel, the verbal poetical texture, and not the tale. Almost every sentence he wrote calls attention to itself as sentence, as precisely crafted crystal artifice, as self-reflexive reference prompting us again and again to remember that we are experiencing flamboyant fiction, not flat fact. True, Humbert Humbert kills Cue with his chum Chum, but he also kills, or at least deeply challenges, many prose conventions with his startling style. His language (and Nabokov's behind it) is self-consciously ornate and self-referential in its very virtuosity, even though it is supposedly hastily scribbled down in 56 days. In a sense, it is a language that through its verbal flash and glitter parodies traditional novelistic language, the virtually transparent language of a Hemingway or Steinbeck, Balzac or Beattie. We need only think of its delicate alliterative interlacing, internal half-rhymes, and at times even Hopkinsesque sprung rhythm ("There, she sat down on the edge of the bed, swaying a little, speaking in dove-dull, long-drawn tones" [122]), its wealth of resonant puns and portmanteau words and anagrams and double entendres (Hum reads a child development book with the "biblical title" *Know Your Own Daughter* [174]), and its myriad other sorts of word play (a single example must suffice: at Pavor Manor, Cue claims that he's "dying for a smoke," and Humbert reminds him: "You're dying anyway" [296]).

Nabokov signals the fictionality of his fiction in many additional ways. We have already discussed his use of such recurring literary-historical conceits as mirrors and reflections, doubles, sports, plays-within-plays, parodies of general genres and specific works, serious allusions, and name games, all present in what is supposed to be a quickly written and unrevised manuscript. To those we might add regular switches between first- and third-person points of view and a proliferation of Chinese-puzzle-box patterning, the repetition of key situations or phrases: Charlotte's note to Hum in part 1 is matched by Dolly's note to Hum in part 2; Charlotte's automobile accident in part 1 parallels Humbert's at the end of part 2; the novel opens and concludes with the word "Lolita." Especially important in this respect is "the long hairy arm of Coincidence" (105), the presence of which in classical tragedy or nineteenth-century naturalist fiction would flag the existence of fate, but the presence of which in *Lolita* flags only the existence of its jocular author. The string of coincidences in the book is downright mind-boggling, and far too long to strike us as anything but cleverly contrived. Some cases in point: McCoo's house just happens to burn down as Humbert arrives in Ramsdale; McCoo just happens to know a Mrs. Haze, friend of his wife, who would be happy to accommodate Humbert; Charlotte just happens to get run over as she is about to blow the whistle on Humbert; Dolly just happens to be on a hike when her mother dies, and hence not in a position to hear about it from anyone except her lover-to-be; the title of the drama in which Dolly acts just happens to be the same as the name of the hotel in which Dolly and Humbert consummate their relationship; Charlotte's house number just happens to be 342, the same as Dolly and Hum's room at the Enchanted Hunters, and the same as the sum of hotels and motels in which they stay during their first year on the road.

Cue's murder scene, foreshadowed heavily through the text, collects most of these self-reflexive elements together into one unhinged chapter. We discover everything from nods toward such genres as the Poeian Gothic story and the classic fairy tale in terms of the chapter's location (Pavor Manor, Grimm Road) and atmosphere (portending thunderstorm, ominous shadows), through its concentration on doubleness, mirrors, marksmanship, puns, and parodies, to Clare the Impredictable's drawn-out burlesque of a death fit simultaneously for a Charlie Chaplin film and an Elizabethan revenge drama. Even Humbert must wryly register, as Cue lies in a purple heap on the landing, how tidily the book's last long scene pulls together so many diverse elements in the text: "This, I said to myself, was the end of the ingenious play staged for me by Quilty" (305). Another work-within-a-work, it is also an ingenious play staged for the reader by Nabokov.

It is surely, to quote Hum as he drives away, "a novel experience" (306). Or, better yet, it is the experience of reading a novel.

So Dolly is Humbert's plaything, Humbert is Quilty's, both Humbert and Quilty are McFate's, the reader is the writer's, and the writer continually asks us to recall the fact that he is an omniscient and omnipotent entity within the narrative cosmos he has created. "Imagine me," Humbert demands of his reader at one point. "I shall not exist if you do not imagine me" (129). The same holds true for Nabokov, who makes sure we never forget him by perpetually planting signposts directing us beyond his realistic characters and settings and right to the impish author himself, reclining at his novelistic control panel in his funhouse of fiction. Revealingly, Dr. Ray in the foreword often seems more interested in the novelist's skills than in the psychiatrist's, and his tone oscillates between shrill pompous proclamations ("*Lolita* deals with situations and emotions that would remain exasperatingly vague to the reader had their expression been etiolated by means of platitudinous evasions" [4]) and self-righteous homilies ("A desperate honesty that throbs through [Humbert's] confession does not absolve him from sins of diabolical cunning" [5]). Ray speaks of Humbert's mask, "through which two hypnotic eyes seem to glow" (3), but those eyes belong as much to Nabokov as they do to the protagonist's "authentic" self. And what about the Farlows's dogs, Cavell and Melampus? Only Nabokov would have had the smarts, we realize if we stop to think about it for second, to give the dogs those names—certainly not the prosaic Farlows themselves. Cavell is from the Portuguese word *cavallo*, or horse, Melampus from the prophet in Greek mythology who understood the language of dogs, and Nabokov christened them, as Alfred Appel, Jr., points out in his annotations, after the dogs of a famous person—quite possibly Lord Byron, though after the fact Nabokov was unsure himself (373).

Here is a writer who playfully invents works composed by nonexistent writers (*La Beauté Humaine*, the book with the sexy photos he lifts from his father's hotel library as a child, doesn't exist any more than its author, Pichon, whose name suggests *nichon*, the French slang for the female breast [11]); expects us to remember that Hum first met Dolly at the house of the widow Haze so that we might smile three-fourths of a novel later when we realize he loses her at the motor court of the widow Hays (on, if we are paying even more careful attention, July Fourth, Dolly's Independence Day); and mischievously toys with our readerly expectations ("A few words more about Mrs. Humbert while the going is good," he taunts us at the opening of chapter 19, since "a bad accident is to happen quite soon" [79]). Clearly, it is not only the protagonist who means it when he says, "I suppose I am especially susceptible to the magic of games" (233).

Humbert Humbert traverses America's roads, always longing to fulfill his lust and possess his princess. This much is obvious. But the reader of *Lolita* also traverses the highways and byways of Nabokov's text, always longing to fulfill the narrative's networks, constellations, harmonies. Hum's desire for Dolly thus metamorphoses into our own for decoding the text's vaudevillian moves. Yet Hum eventually comes to learn that he can never completely claim his ideal, can never completely reduce it to the state of static object, while we eventually come to learn that we can never completely claim the text as our own since it remains nothing if not a slip, slide, and perpetual process. With the author peeking out puckishly from behind every sentence, every alliterative stutter and lyrical rhythm, every gag and game, it is more than appropriate that Nabokov end his afterword with a discussion of language lost and found: "My private tragedy, which cannot, and indeed should not, be anybody's concern, is that I had to abandon my natural idiom, my untrammeled, rich, and infinitely docile Russian tongue for a second-rate brand of English, devoid of any of those apparatuses—the baffling mirror, the black velvet backdrop, the implied associations and traditions—which the native illusionist, frac-tails flying, can magically use to transcend the heritage in his own way" (316–17). The last line of *Lolita* thereby leaves us with the comic illusionist stuck in a tragic state, with a pervasive sense of haunting nostalgia that is at the same time undercut by bright alliteration, with more self-referential mirrors, more mentions of associations and traditions that need to be surpassed, an emphasis on language that is at least as important as the emphasis on a single melancholy human being—and, perhaps above all else, that splendid enduring image of author as droll magician, with his ability to enchant, to entertain, to teach, and to downright dazzle.

CONCLUSION: *LOLITA* AS A JANUS TEXT

Another way to put this is to say that the afterword's last sentence is emblematic of the novel as a whole in its momentous sense of contradiction. Within it beats a very real feeling of longing alongside a very real comic impulse, a concentration on the artifice of language alongside a concentration on the sad emotions of an isolated and exiled human being, a celebration of the idea of a traditional mother tongue alongside a need to move beyond the idea of tradition, a warm humane tenderness alongside a cool cerebral self-reflexivity, a representation of the author as pyrotechnic magician alongside a representation of the author as romantic who can break your heart. The sentence, like the text itself, perpetually and profoundly peers two ways at once.

A fitting icon for this narrative move might be the head of the Roman god Janus. Most ancient king of Italy when alive, Janus upon his death became guardian of doorways to houses and gateways to cities. Because of his role as protector, he had two faces, one on the front of his head and one on the back. Hence he could concurrently keep an eye on things before and behind him. Having also played a part in the universe's creation, Janus became the god of beginnings and was invoked at the start of various enterprises, including the launch of the new year—thus his month, January. Because of his forever forward-looking nature, he became the god of endings as well. So during the Renaissance his two faces became symbolic of past and future in allegories about time.

In an analogous manner, *Lolita* gazes in two directions at once. It promises the coarse obscenity of pornography only to deliver the pristine purity of a moral message. It presents Humbert Humbert as a baleful beast only to give us a host of reasons for sympathizing with him, or at least in some small degree understanding him. We find Dolly both an abrasive brat and a poignant victim, both Hum's pawn and his queen, and we find Quilty a fully-rounded character in addition to being a menacing metaphor for universal McFatedness. *Lolita* provides us with an optic through which to read with a deeply ethical, even purgatorial purview, yet amorally undoes the authority of an ethical interpretation by means of a deeply renegade comic urge. The book is a serious, sad, and even nostalgic one that is also gamesome, witty, and calculatingly analytical. It purports to be, and in many ways is, a mimetic text that reflects a resonantly three-dimensional postwar America peopled by complexly three-dimensional characters, and yet also assumes the role of brilliant self-conscious metafiction concerned with its own status as fiction, a trompe l'oeil text that calls attention to its own deceptive nature. Its three-dimensional world is thereby revealed to be a novelistic illusion, those three-dimensional characters no more than the author's puppets and playthings. *Lolita*'s language claims to render reality limpidly while also announcing itself as unadulterated artifice, hence troubling the very notion of limpid rendering (not to mention "reality" itself). The novel is highly untraditional at the same instant it is thoroughly and extensively grounded in literary tradition. It is highly original at the same instant it is exceptionally generic. It seems to partake of one kind of genre only to turn in midsentence toward another. It appears to be a stable text, but on closer inspection it becomes a strikingly metamorphic one.

Nor do these pairs of elements exist along an either/or axis. That is to say, our job as critics is not to choose between these binary terms, prioritize them, or suggest that one element in each set is in fact the sovereign one. Nabokov's novel is not merely one thing or another, our purpose as readers not merely to decide which it is and why. Rather, *Lolita* is often at least two things at once, and it asserts each member of each pair of contradictory terms with the same force. By generating this disturbingly both/and perspective, it calls for a strategy of double-reading on our part, a strategy that overturns ideas of singularity, hierarchy, and even traditionally stable interpretation itself. We thereby enter the limitless labyrinthine landscape of indeterminacy and undecidability: the landscape, that is, of the postmodern.

Indeed the most significant Janus gaze within the text is the one that simultaneously looks back toward a modern orientation and ahead toward a postmodern one. While Nabokov would have neither understood *Lolita* in this manner nor approved in the slightest of our increasingly general discussion of his book, it might nonetheless be instructive for us as readers to tempt his specter's wrath. Before we begin, we should understand that the labels "modern" and "postmodern" refer less to rigidly defined historical periods than to somewhat slippery states of mind. Although it is true that these states of mind have surfaced at different times in different places throughout the course of Western culture, it is also true that they have gained dominance at specific moments in specific sites. Thus we can begin to grasp how it is accurate to assert *both* that François Rabelais's *Gargantua and Pantagruel* or Laurence Sterne's *Tristram Shandy* evince a mischievous and dislocating postmodern impetus at least as radical and intense as that evinced by the drastically disruptive and self-reflexive stories in John Barth's *Lost in the Funhouse* or Robert Coover's *Pricksongs and Descants, and* that such textual (and existential) disruption and self-reflexivity came to pervade Western culture shortly after World War II.

How might we more precisely formulate these modes of consciousness? To start, we must briefly introduce a third state of mind, the "premodern." If premodern consciousness frames its world in terms of master narratives, or grand fictions that lend shape and substance to people's lives (the idea of humanism within the Renaissance, or those of symmetry, order, and reason within neoclassicism), modern consciousness senses a potential loss of master narratives. By the late nineteenth century, many felt that developments in geology had begun to shrink humankind's position in time, while developments in astronomy had begun to shrink its position in space. Darwinian biology seemed only to underscore this sense of existential displacement, dislodging our privileged place in the Great Chain of Being and reconceptualizing us, not as beings with angelic potential but simply as higher-order animals shaped by heredity and environment. This notion was reinforced at the turn of the century by Freud's immensely dark view of the human psyche, with his emphasis on a language of desire, irrationality, and repressed violence, and by the horrible dimensions of destruction wrought by the first world conflict, from the mass killing power of the machine gun to the hideous results of mustard gas and trench warfare. Add to these a poignant feeling of rootlessness brought on by the proliferation of the automobile and airplane, an intense awareness of a contracting globe and increasing sense of cultural relativism brought on by the invention of photography and film, the telephone and the radio. The result was a striking feeling of dislocation and disorder in literary, artistic, and musical projects. We need think only of the fractured utterances of Eliot's *The Waste Land* and Joyce's *Ulysses* and the fragmented shards of Braque's and Picasso's cubist collages or the atonal compositions of Arnold Schönberg. The predictability of Newtonian physics burst into Einsteinian spatiotemporality in more than just the laboratory. Although Einstein never advocated a thoroughgoing relativism, maintaining instead that the universe still contained immutable laws of motion, temporality, and causality, the concept of absolute knowledge nonetheless evaporated in the popular mind before the realization that the position of the observer (be it in terms of events, culture, or philosophy) was relative to the thing observed.

This, we should take a moment to remind ourselves, is the progressively industrialized and urbanized world of scientific, philosophical, political, and aesthetic shocks into which Nabokov was born. And it is a world that leads to a sometimes desperate, sometimes liberating awareness on the part of many of its inhabitants that the long-standing stability of tradition has begun to give way under a new network of complex pressures. Hence a hunger for the cohesion and coherence that customs and conventions once provided arises side by side with an energetic and even at times optimistic avant-garde attempt (as Ezra Pound asserted in his imagist manifesto) to make it new. Amid the geography of modern literature we locate Joyce, Woolf, and Faulkner rethinking narrative, e. e. cummings, Wallace Stevens, and William Carlos Williams rethinking poetry, but we also locate Yeats on a lifelong pilgrimage for a unified private mythology, Hemingway for a code of behavior, Eliot for the great gift of tradition itself. We locate, to put it slightly differently, a group of creators who saw their work not only as an artistic revolution but also as an existential last stand against encroaching cosmic chaos, as a way (to paraphrase Eliot in the final section of *The Waste Land*) to shore up their culture's fragments against its ruins. Through the development of elaborate symbolic structures, these creative pioneers attempted to encircle and tame what they perceived to be a frenzied universe.

No doubt their texts at first glance appear almost as confusing as the chaotic cosmos aswarm beyond them, but on closer study and extended meditation they yield a deep sense of order and meaning beneath their seeming voids of meaninglessness. Beneath the sometimes bewildering shards of *The Waste Land*, for instance, we discern the ordering principle of Jessie Weston's scholarly work on ritual and romance, and beneath the sometimes confounding stream-of-consciousness and linguistic hoopla that composes Joyce's *Ulysses*, we make out Homeric myth, that oldest icon of Western heritage. Beneath those cubist collages by Braque and Picasso we recognize traditional human forms, and beneath that cacophony of Schönberg's atonal music we perceive the patterning rules of serialism.

Modern consciousness, to rephrase the case, develops a number of responses to the turbulent situation in which it finds itself by seeking to generate a sense of underlying aesthetic and philosophical design in the artifacts it produces. Postmodern consciousness, on the other hand, can't find a response adequate to the mind-bending situation in which it finds itself. The idea of the master narrative hence detonates into a series of highly-relativized micronarratives, one just as valid (or invalid) as another. We come across many who, in the wake of World War II, with its staggering 40 million-plus casualties, sense a new series of scientific, philosophical, political, and aesthetic shock waves rolling through the culture. The planet spirals into a postindustrial crisis of technology with nuclear disaster becoming not simply the subject of recent science fiction but a real possibility in an increasingly science fictional world. Visions of the mushroom cloud above vaporized Hiroshima (not to mention the extensive death machines of Nazi concentration camps) burn themselves into our cultural memory. The space program commences, soon sending us back photos of our planet from orbit, a small blue ball in an infinite inky sea, and yet, not long after humankind reaches the moon, the frontiers of space and of NASA begin to recede, and we witness that heart-stopping fireball called the *Challenger*. Meanwhile, our global village slowly awakens to the staggering degree of environmental damage it has heaped on itself, the ozone layer dissipating almost as quickly as our natural resources, even as the righteous paranoia associated with the Cold War and the

Communist Scare spread from Korea, to Vietnam, and beyond. Television retrains our perception, shortening it, thinning it, and speeding it up, while computers redefine the depth and degree of information around us, making access to that information *the* new central form of power. We discover ourselves having to think about subjects we never had to think about before, from organ transplants to the rapid commodification of art, entropy to white noise, smart drugs to chaos theory, artificial intelligence to conurbanization, toxic waste to world famine, rampant overpopulation to the effects of future shock on our increasingly shaken psyches.

Postmodern consciousness, then, to employ theorist Jean-François Lyotard's point of view on the matter, tries to present the unpresentable, whether it be in the gray half-world of Beckett's aptly named novella *The Unnamable*, in which the protagonist is not sure where he/it is, who he/it is, or even *if* he/it is; or video artist Nam June Paik's vast walls of television screens playing unpredictable and random sets of images in a kind of cyberblitz; or the band Sonic Youth's walls of raw industrial noise created by elaborate feedback techniques. We find ourselves exploring a domain that encompasses everything from the Beatles's nonsense sound-collage, *Revolution 9*, replete with soccer cheers, clanging piano, and snippets from Shakespeare recited by John Lennon, to Mark Pauline and the Survival Research Laboratory's posthuman entertainments involving gigantic self-destructing robots, explosions, and shredded animal carcasses. Postmodern consciousness skeptically problematizes everything our culture once took for granted about language and experience—*and* generally delights in the process.

Under postmodern inspection, the universe morphs into pluriverse, the world mutates from (as French theorist Roland Barthes would have it) a *work* into a *text*. That is, the postmodern creates a space where there is no longer an Author-God creating a single meaning but a multidimensional area of ludic activity in which diverse micronarratives, none better or worse than any other, clash, blend, and reform in stimulating and challenging ways. If the appropriate metaphor from physics for modern consciousness is Einsteinian relativity, then the appropriate metaphor from physics for postmodern consciousness is quantum mechanics, a subject that has been around for much of the twentieth century but that has gained increasing popular recognition over the last several decades owing to the appearance of such luminous introductions to the subject as Stephen Hawking's *A Brief History of Time* and Timothy Ferris's *Coming of Age in the Milky Way*. According to this theory, at the submicroscopic level of quanta there exists an oscillating realm where diurnal notions of linearity, causality, temporality, and ontology no longer function with sureness, where violent acausality seems to be the rule. In this dimension, physicist Werner Karl Heisenberg's Uncertainty Principle holds sway, asserting that the observer cannot help affecting the observed. Whether a quanta appears as wave or particle depends completely on the mode by which, and length of time through which, it is observed. The universe thereby becomes a multiverse of statistical probabilities shimmering in and out of existence.

Theorist Brian McHale argues that the cultural dominant (or focusing component of a particular piece of art or way of thinking) changes from a perspective that emphasizes epistemological concerns in modern consciousness to one that emphasizes ontological ones in postmodern. For Andreas Huyssen, postmodern consciousness is the willy-nilly mixture of "high" and "low" culture. And, for Jean Baudrillard, it means nothing less than a kind of cultural schizophrenia in which any hope of attaining the real has collapsed into an infinite regression of appearances: simulations of simulations of simulations. Whichever construction we follow (and we should keep in mind that these are *only* constructions, provisional stories—our position being far too close to the object we are examining to hope for much else), we detect in the geography of its literature Julio Cortázar composing a novel whose chapters can be shuffled like playing cards and can be read in various ways to arrive at various meanings; Kathy Acker producing "original" texts by pla(y)giarizing others; and Thomas Pynchon applauding ideas of entropy, irrelevance, and waste in his fiction while eschewing the very kinds of static, closed systems that Yeats, Eliot, and Hemingway sought with such earnestness. We detect, to put it simply, a group of artists who see their art as a celebration of decentralization, diversification, and demassification, whose works display little tolerance for borders of any kind. In reaction to modern notions of desperate purpose, experimental design, mastery, synthesis, and a sense of tradition, the postmodern enjoys festive play, experimental designlessness, anarchy, deconstruction, and a devilish demythologization of tradition.

In this context *Lolita* becomes an amphibious work of art, equally able to inhabit the fairly firm land of the modern and the amorphous sea of the postmodern. It easily changes its temperature with its surroundings, becoming this or that depending on its reader's sensibilities and Nabokov's mood on a specific page, in a specific paragraph, even in a specific sentence. If we ponder the situation for a moment, we realize this novel clearly maintains a strong allegiance to the modern existential pilgrimage for complex design amid disorder, shape beneath shapelessness. We need only remember those carefully orchestrated systems of ironic meaning that cluster beneath the seeming scramble of details during the cryptogrammic paper chase, or the elaborate foreshadowing, narrative balances, and intricate echoes that compose the apparently straightforward (and allegedly quickly written) realistic manuscript we're exploring. And if Joyce employed the metaphor of Homeric myth to contour *Ulysses*, then we may say that Nabokov employed the metaphor of lepidoptery to contour *Lolita*. Moreover, Joyce is only one drop in a vast pool of references to previous literary and artistic works to which Nabokov, so instinctively rooted in heritage, so vitally concerned with mastery and synthesis, alludes.

"I am thinking of aurochs and angels, the secret of durable pigments, prophetic sonnets, the refuge of art," Humbert Humbert, the narrator whose unreliability raises essential modern questions about knowing, whose false double name signals the essential modern problemization of selfhood, writes on the very brink of the grave. "And this is the only immortality you and I may share, my Lolita" (309). Remarkably, his last thoughts don't have to do with politics or philosophy, his highly relative sense of right and wrong. They have to do instead with the defining power of aesthetics, with the durable pigments of cave paintings like those at Lascaux that inspired Picasso, the prophetic sonnets of those like Shakespeare that aspired (as does Humbert's project) to immortalize the writer's lover. Aurochs, extinct

European wild oxen, and angels, nonexistent beings, are as elusive in Humbert's mind as the object of his desperately serious quest, his desire to metamorphose his darling Dolly from the impermanence of aging flesh into the eternally pristine refuge of timeless art. Thus does Hum (and, on a different plane, Nabokov himself) attempt to enclose and temper chaotic experience in an aesthetic move akin to that of Wallace Stevens in a quintessentially modernist poem like "Anecdote of the Jar." There, the narrator places a jar on an overgrown hillside in Tennessee and, in the blink of an eye, the presence of that jar utterly transforms the terrain around it. A human artifact abruptly restricts and controls the wilderness. Or, in other words, the work of art by its very existence creates a sense of cosmos out of chaos. Emblematic of modern consciousness in general, the jar, a product of sheer imagination, shapes and orders the commotion of everyday reality in the same way that Stevens's poem (and Humbert's book, and Nabokov's) does.

But this is only a corner of the overall picture. After all, as we have seen, *Lolita* also disturbs our assumptions about the nature of words and worlds, giving these no more than shifting and provisional values. In a sense, it just as well creates chaos out of cosmos as it does cosmos out of chaos. Its tone is highly complex and ambiguous, altering quickly, unpredictably, and often within the confines of a single sentence, making it exceedingly difficult for us to read through Humbert's (and Nabokov's) ironic stance to any solid bedrock of meaning. Furthermore, as we have witnessed on repeated occasions, part of Nabokov's purpose is to generate constructs that thwart simple and simplistic readings, be they Freudian, Marxist, or otherwise commensurately constrictive. His text shuns inert, hermetically-sealed systems while joyfully opening ludic spaces of mutually contradictory possibilities. Aporia, or irreconcilable paradox, therefore beats at the heart of this novel, which frequently holds up binary levels of "reality" (moral/amoral, serious/comic, epistemological/ontological literary/pop, realistic/artificial) as equally viable. In a deconstructive blueprint, *Lolita* sets forth conflicting ways of perceiving the pluriverse. By doing so, it undermines and then topples traditional ideas of hierarchy and univocality. The consequence is a polyphonically delightful, polymorphously perverse, and playfully anarchistic demythologization of everything from love to truth, freewill to mimesis, knowledge to being. Nabokov's novel presents a continual collision of worlds, a perpetual indeterminacy of meaning. It metaphorically Lichtensteinizes Botticelli while emphasizing how any conventional sense of the "real" has imploded into a mirrory postmodern funhouse of cartoonish simulacra.

Lolita thereby marks a crucial instant in Western consciousness. On the one hand, it forms a fond (and yet frequently frolicsome) summary of the modern moment in literature, looking back toward the stylistic experiments and somber philosophical explorations of supreme fictions by the likes of Joyce, Woolf, Proust, and even Nabokov himself in the novel *Pnin*, his poignant and relatively straightforward portrait of a Russian émigré teaching in New York State, his pre-*Lolita* study of consciousness and conscience. On the other hand, it forms one of the first deliberately deconstructive stirrings of the postmodern moment in literature, looking ahead to the linguistic and ontological trips, stutters, and falls of skeptical surfictions by the likes of Donald Barthelme, Italo Calvino, Gilbert Sorrentino, and—again—Nabokov himself in the follow-up novel to *Lolita*, the playfully extreme poem-cum-academentic-analysis *Pale Fire*. It asks us what the limits are to knowledge, what we can know, how we can know it, with what certainty, while at the same time asking us what constitutes a world, a self, a text, what sort of boundaries exist between worlds, between selves, between texts, what the natures of our existences (and those of books) are. No longer quite comfortable with the beautiful motionless aestheticism of Ford Maddox Ford's *The Good Soldier* (another novel foregrounding rich narratorial unreliability) or with the relentless existential seriousness of Dostoevsky's *Notes from Underground*, and yet not quite comfortable either with the near-complete dehumanization in a text like Alain Robbe-Grillet's *Jealousy* (which effectively effaces its narrator while generating a degree-zero style) or with the relentless commotion of William Burroughs's cut-up novels, Nabokov's *Lolita* occupies a narrative space that is all edge. It marks a technical and philosophical limit, an historical hesitation as well as a creative springboard that will launch such diverse writers as William Gass, Alasdair Gray, Guy Davenport, and T. C. Boyle into fresh and unexpected fictional dimensions.

Lolita is nothing, then, if not a text that forces questions rather than answers, endorses processes over products, proclaims inconclusiveness rather than conclusion. Through such a strategy, it reopens our perceptions to the world(s) around us rather than presenting us with the stultifying and standardizing vision of this dogma or that. It offers a fictional case and case of fiction that even go so far as to interrogate the separateness of such concepts as modern and postmodern, and, ultimately, the entire enterprise concerned with literary periodization and historiography. Hardly the narratologically conservative product of a political and philosophical reactionary, as some recent (and sadly uninformed) critics have asserted, *Lolita* is the narratologically radical product of a richly independent political and philosophical iconoclast. And this, in the final analysis, may help account for *Lolita*'s status as a masterwork.

Of course the term *masterwork* itself has lately come under postmodern scrutiny. Theorists have been quick and correct to underscore the cultural and aesthetic relativism involved in defining such a misleadingly "objective" (and obviously masculine) term. Related to it is the correspondingly troublesome concept of "the canon," or constellation of "masterworks." A word originally associated with the authorized list of books belonging to the Christian Bible and with the names of saints authorized by the Church, *canon* currently refers as well to the "authorized" list of "masterworks" associated with a particular writer or period of literary history. But who, theorists ask warily, does the authorizing? Along what lines? And what are the consequences of such choices? Often the answer has been that white, Anglo-Saxon, heterosexual males in positions of institutional power have done the authorizing, and done so to perpetuate the heritage they themselves have been taught to perpetuate. The less-than-surprising outcome has been (whether knowingly, if we are of a conspiratorial disposition, or unknowingly, if we are not) to make one part of society's works, interests, and values central to the study of literature while reducing those of others to the depreciated status of "marginal," "minor," or "extracanonical." Hence, for example, while the early modern "canon" for many years included the "masterworks" of such magnificent writers as Eliot, Joyce, Hemingway, Faulkner, and Pound, such talented and significant creators as Marianne Moore, Zora Neale Hurston, Langston Hughes, Nathanael West, and Black Elk were excluded from examination. The result, surely, has been a culture the poorer for it, although in the last decades of the twentieth century the situation has happily begun to shift toward the more inclusive.

With this in mind, though, how can we even *begin* to claim the status of "masterwork" for *Lolita*? Perhaps in a sense we can't, and perhaps in a sense we shouldn't—not, at least, if we fail to acknowledge the cultural and aesthetic relativism informing our judgment. If, however, we *do* acknowledge it—and speedily concede both the provisional nature of our assessment and the personal pragmatic fact that we simply happen to *enjoy* this text aesthetically, emotionally, and intellectually (thus defining it for us, here, now, as a "masterwork," even while we are glad to grant that for others it might not be)—perhaps we can proceed and make our qualified claim. While doing so, we might also recall that as we approached the serious study of literature for the first time in high school, we frequently heard that "masterwork" simply denotes a piece of art that keeps us coming back, and it is difficult to argue with such a straightforward and commonsense definition as this, although we clearly must admit that different pieces of art keep different people coming back for different reasons at different times.

In the case of *Lolita*, and in the case of *this* author and many critics like him, it is enough to say, here, now, that a "masterwork" is an aesthetically pleasing imaginative gesture that continues to reveal intriguing insights to us about itself, ourselves, and the pluriverse we inhabit. It makes us feel and think deeply about the nature of existence, makes us wonder about our lives and our worlds, stimulates us to challenge our conventional assumptions about the way the big things work, and (to hearken back to Gertrude Stein on the subject) releases us from the perceptual vises in which our dull heads tend to be locked. It is enough to say, now, here, that we know we have discovered a masterwork when we have discovered a whole book about which we can easily write a whole book, and yet at the conclusion of this pleasurable process realize we have only chicken-scratched the proverbial surface. It is enough to say that we know we have discovered a masterwork when we have discovered a text that will surely invite us back for further visits, and surely reward its invitation with fresh and intriguing thoughts, fine and involved disclosures, and full and impressive emotions. And, if this is so, then we have without a doubt found a masterwork in the breathtakingly textured intricacies and resonantly rich relevancies of Vladimir Nabokov's *Lolita*.

Notes

Chapter 1

1. Frederick R. Karl, *American Fictions 1940–1980* (New York: Harper & Row, 1983), 176. He mentions a fourth metaphor as well, less helpful for our purposes here: "Burroughs's hallucinatory, drug-induced universe." All four, however, will inform *Lolita,* even the last, which manifests itself in Humbert's surreal "cryptogrammic paper chase."

2. Brian Boyd, *Vladimir Nabokov: The American Years* (Princeton: Princeton University Press, 1991), 503, 553; hereafter cited in text. Many of the biographical facts from this chapter and from the chronology of Nabokov's life come from this book and its prequel: *Vladimir Nabokov: The Russian Years* (Princeton: Princeton University Press, 1990); hereafter cited in text.

Chapter 2

1. Namely *Tyrants Destroyed and Other Stories, Pnin, Pale Fire, Transparent Things,* and *Look at the Harlequins!*

2. A multidisciplinary group that flourished just prior to and during the 1920s, Russian formalists, such as Boris Eichenbaum, Vladimir Propp, and Roman Jakobson, stressed the idea of form over content. More important, as Victor Shklovsky argues in his seminal essay, "Art as Technique," "Art exists that one may recover the sensation of life; it exists to make one feel things, to make the stone *stony.* The purpose of art is to impart the sensation of things as they are perceived and not as they are known. The technique of art is to make objects 'unfamiliar,' to make forms difficult, to increase the difficulty and length of perception because the process of perception is an aesthetic end in itself and must be prolonged." *Russian Formalist Criticism: Four Essays,* ed. and trans. Lee T. Lemon and Marion J. Reis. (Lincoln: University of Nebraska Press, 1965), 12.

Chapter 3

1. Vladimir Nabokov, *Strong Opinions* (New York: Vintage, 1973), 16; hereafter cited in text as *SO*.

Chapter 4

1. Vladimir Nabokov and Edmund Wilson, *The Nabokov-Wilson Letters, 1940–1971,* ed. Simon Karlinsy (New York: Viking, 1977), 296, 298.

2. Interview with John Coleman, *Spectator* 6 (November 1959), 619.

3. Vladimir Nabokov, *Lolita: A Screenplay* (New York: McGraw-Hill, 1974), 127. Kubrick apparently found the scene too self-indulgent and superfluous.

4. D. H. Lawrence, "Fenimore Cooper's Leatherstocking Novels," in *Studies in Classic American Literature* (New York: Doubleday, 1923), 73. The fourth trait, which the often-resigned Humbert doesn't evince, is stoicism.

5. This distinction between *chronos* and *kairos* is borrowed from Frank Kermode's *The Sense of an Ending: Studies in the Theory of Fiction* (New York: Oxford University Press, 1967), 47–48.

6. Edgar Allan Poe, *The Complete Tales and Poems of Edgar Allan Poe* (New York: Modern Library, 1938), 894.

7. Christina Tekiner, for instance, goes so far as to ingeniously argue in her article "Time in *Lolita*" that neither Humbert's final meeting with Dolly Schiller nor his murder of Quilty ever actually happened but were fabricated by Humbert in prison, where he was serving time not for murder but for statutory rape and carrying a minor across state lines. Much of Tekiner's argument is based on a possible gaff in Humbert's date keeping. For more, see *Modern Fiction Studies* 25 (1979): 463–69.

8. This might be a good point to pause and limn the chronology of these odysseys, as well as the full time frame of the book. Hum is born in 1910 and meets Dolly, herself born in 1935, in 1947, having moved to the Haze house in May of that year. At their first meeting, Dolly is 12 years old and in seventh grade and has been living with Charlotte in Charlotte's late mother-in-law's house in Ramsdale since 1945, when they moved from Pisky after Harold Haze's death. In June 1947 Charlotte decides to send Dolly to Camp Q, and Hum and Charlotte marry a month later while Dolly is still away. During that same month, Charlotte discovers Hum's diary and is killed by Beale's car on the way to post a letter that would have alerted the world to her discovery.

Hum picks up Dolly at camp and they begin their first cross-country trek, which lasts from August 1947 to August 1948. They then settle at 14 Thayer Street in Beardsley, where Dolly re-enters school. In June 1949, a week before *The Enchanted Hunters* play goes up, Hum pulls Dolly from Beardsley and they begin their second cross-country trek. On 4 July 1949, Lo is stolen away from Hum by Quilty, and from 5 July through 18 November 1949 Hum retraces his steps in search of the couple. In November he returns to Beardsley, and from November 1949 through November 1951 he hires an incompetent detective who turns up little. Meantime, he has another mental breakdown in the winter of 1949, the same time Dolly leaves Quilty. Hum meets Rita in the summer of 1950 and travels with her until the summer of 1952.

On 22 September 1952 he receives a letter from Dolly asking for money, and he traces her to Coalmont. From there he goes to Briceland to find Quilty through his dentist-uncle, and his trail leads to Pavor Manor, where Hum kills his nemesis and is shortly thereafter arrested. He begins quickly writing his book over the next 56 days, dying on 16 November 1952. Dolly dies about a month later on 25 December 1952.

9. Martin Amis, "*Lolita* Reconsidered," *Atlantic,* September 1992, 119–20; hereafter cited in text.

10. Thomas Pynchon, "Introduction," in *Slow Learner* (New York: Little, Brown, 1984), 5, 15.

11. Vladimir Nabokov, *Nikolai Gogol* (New York: New Directions, 1944), 142.

12. Lionel Trilling, "The Last Lover" in *Encounter* 11 (October 1958), 19.

13. Richard Pearce, "Nabokov's Black(Hole) Humor: *Lolita* and *Pale Fire*," in *Comic Relief: Humor in Contemporary American Literature,* ed. Sarah Blacher Cohen (Urbana: University of Illinois Press, 1978), 30, 31.

Chapter 5

1. Harold Bloom, "Introduction," in *Vladimir Nabokov's "Lolita,"* ed. Harold Bloom (New York: Chelsea House Publishers, 1987), 1.

2. Interestingly enough, however, Nabokov did not think that Carroll's "invented language share[d] any roots" with his own (*SO,* 81).

3. Mikhail Bakhtin, *Problems of Dostoevsky's Poetics,* trans. R. W. Rotsel (Ann Arbor: Ardis, 1973), 87.

Bibliography

Primary Works

Novels

All Russian works from 1920 to 1940 were published under pseudonyms, usually V. Sirin.

Ada or Ardor: A Family Chronicle. New York: McGraw-Hill, 1969.

Bend Sinister. New York: Henry Holt, 1947.

Camera obscura. Published serially in *Sovremennye zapiski,* 1932. Translated by VN as *Laughter in the Dark.* Indianapolis: Bobbs-Merrill, 1938.

Dar. Published serially in *Sovremennye zapiski,* 1937–38. Translated by Michael Scammell and Dmitri Nabokov with VN as *The Gift.* New York: Chekhov, 1952.

Korol', dama, valet. Berlin: Slovo, 1928. Translated by Dmitri Nabokov with VN as *King, Queen, Knave.* New York: McGraw-Hill, 1968.

Lolita. Paris: Olympia, 1955. New York: Putnam's, 1958. Best edition: *The Annotated Lolita.* Edited by Alfred Appel, Jr. New York: McGraw-Hill, 1970. Full text with superb introduction and line-by-line annotations.

Look at the Harlequins! New York: McGraw-Hill, 1974.

Mashen'ka. Berlin: Slovo, 1926. Translated by Michael Glenny with VN as *Mary.* New York: McGraw-Hill, 1970.

Otchayanie. Berlin: Petropolis, 1936. Translated by VN. New York: Putnam's, 1966.

Pale Fire. New York: Putnam's, 1962.

Pnin. New York: Doubleday, 1957.

Podvig. Published serially in *Sovremennye zapiski,* 1931–32. Translated by Dmitri Nabokov with VN as *Glory.* New York: McGraw-Hill, 1971.

Priglashenie na kazn'. Paris: Dom Knigi, 1938. Translated by Dmitri Nabokov and VN as *Invitation to a Beheading.* New York: Putnam's, 1959.

The Real Life of Sebastian Knight. Norfolk, Conn.: New Directions, 1941.

Transparent Things. New York: McGraw-Hill, 1972.

Zashchita Luzhina. Berlin: Slovo, 1930. Translated by Michael Scammel with VN as *The Defense.* New York: Putnam's, 1964.

Shorter Fiction

Details of a Sunset and Other Stories. Translated by Dmitri Nabokov and VN. New York: McGraw-Hill, 1976.

Nabokov's Dozen: A Collection of Thirteen Stories. New York: Doubleday, 1958.

Nabokov's Quartet. New York: Phaedra, 1966. Stories.

Nine Stories. Norfolk, Conn.: New Directions, 1947.

A Russian Beauty and Other Stories. Translated by Dmitri Nabokov and VN. New York: McGraw-Hill, 1973.

Soglyadatai. Published serially in *Sovremennye zapiski,* 1930. Translated by Dmitri Nabokov with VN as *The Eye.* New York: Phaedra, 1965.

Tyrants Destroyed and Other Stories. Translated by Dmitri Nabokov with VN. New York: McGraw-Hill, 1975.

Vesna v Fialte i drugie rasskazy. New York: Chekhov, 1956. Stories.

Vozvrashchenie Chorba. Berlin: Slovo, 1930. Stories and poems.

Poetry and Drama

See Michael Juliar's bibliography (cited below) for a full listing.

Izobretenie Val'sa published in *Russki zapiski* (November 1938). Translated by Dmitri Nabokov with VN as *The Waltz Invention: A Play in Three Acts.* New York: Phaedra, 1966.

Lolita: A Screenplay. New York: McGraw-Hill, 1974.

The Man from USSR and Other Plays. Translated by Dmitri Nabokov. New York: Harcourt Brace Jovanovich, 1984.

Poems and Problems. New York: McGraw-Hill, 1970.

Nonfiction

Nabokov published more than 80 scholarly articles, reviews, letters, and chess problems and at least 20 pieces on lepidoptera. See Michael Juliar's bibliography for details.

Bibliography

Conclusive Evidence. New York: Harper, 1951. Expanded and revised first into *Drugie berega* (New York: Chekhov, 1954), then *Speak, Memory: An Autobiography Revisited* (New York: Putnam's, 1966). Memoir.

Lectures on Literature. Edited by Fredson Bowers. New York: Harcourt Brace Jovanovich, 1980. Followed by *Lectures on Ulysses* (1980), *Lectures on Russian Literature* (1981), and *Lectures on Don Quixote* (1983).

The Nabokov-Wilson Letters: 1940–1971. Edited by Simon Karlinsky. New York: Viking, 1977.

Nikolai Gogol. New York: New Directions, 1944. Critical study.

Translations

In addition to the following, Nabokov published translations of more than a dozen other works. See Michael Juliar's bibliography for details.

Anya v strane chudes. Berlin: Gamayun, 1923. Russian translation of *Alice in Wonderland.*

Eugene Onegin. By Alexander Pushkin. 4 vols. New York: Bollingen, 1964.

A Hero of Our Time. Novel by Mikhail Lermontov. Translated by VN and Dmitri Nabokov. Garden City, N.Y.: Doubleday, 1958.

Lolita (in Russian). New York: Phaedra, 1967.

The Song of Igor's Campaign: An Epic of the Twelfth Century. New York: Random House, 1960.

Three Russian Poets: Translations of Pushkin, Lermontov, and Tyutchev. Norfolk, Conn.: New Directions, 1944.

Secondary Works

Because Nabokov has been written on so extensively, spawning tens of critical studies and dissertations and hundreds of essays, the following is a highly selective bibliography. It may be supplemented by reference to the annual bibliography appearing in the *Vladimir Nabokov Research Newsletter* (1978–84) and the *Nabokovian* (1984–).

Books

Alexandrov, Vladimir E. *Nabokov's Otherworld.* Princeton: Princeton University Press, 1991. Differences between Nabokov's and Humbert's aesthetic and ethical perceptions. Fate as leitmotif. Presence of occult otherworld. Connections with earlier Nabokov works.

Appel, Alfred, Jr. *Nabokov's Dark Cinema.* New York: Oxford University Press, 1974. Graceful discussion of film in *Lolita* and of *Lolita* as a film.

————, and Charles Newman, eds. *Nabokov: Criticism, Reminiscences, Translations, and Tributes.* Evanston, Ill.: Northwestern University Press, 1970. Originally published in *TriQuarterly* 17 (Winter 1970). Uneven but fascinating collection by writers and critics.

Bader, Julia. *Crystal Land: Artifice in Nabokov's English Novels.* Berkeley: University of California Press, 1972. In a study focusing on art and artists in Nabokov's English novels, Bader argues that *Lolita* immortalizes Humbert's passion for his nymphet in art.

Boyd, Brian. *Vladimir Nabokov: The Russians Years.* Princeton: Princeton University Press, 1990. First-rate critical biography covering the period from Nabokov's birth to exile to France.

————. *Vladimir Nabokov: The American Years.* Princeton: Princeton University Press, 1991. Continuation of the above.

Couturier, Maurice. *Nabokov.* Lausanne: Editions l'age d'homme, 1979. Sexuality and poetics in *Lolita.*

Field, Andrew. *Nabokov: His Life in Art.* Boston: Little, Brown, 1967. First book discussing both Russian and English works. Psychological reading of *Lolita.*

————. *Nabokov: His Life in Part.* New York: Viking, 1977. Followed in 1986 by *The Life and Art of Vladimir Nabokov.* New York: Crown. Eccentric, often inaccurate biographies.

Fowler, Douglas. *Reading Nabokov.* Ithaca: Cornell University Press, 1974. Examining the consistency of character types and aesthetic concerns in selected English novels and stories, Fowler argues that Humbert typically maintains his humanity and attains a moral perspective.

Green, Geoffrey. *Freud and Nabokov.* Lincoln: University of Nebraska Press, 1988. Builds on psychoanalytic work of Phyllis A. Roth, J. P. Shute, and others. More about Nabokov than his fictions.

Lee, L. L. *Vladimir Nabokov.* Boston: Twayne, 1976. Introduction. Lee focuses on *Lolita*'s American elements, important allusions, and moral dimension.

Maddox, Lucy. *Nabokov's Novels in English.* Athens: University of Georgia Press, 1983. *Lolita* is the anatomy of a romantic artist's obsession as he hovers between moral and aesthetic standards.

Morton, Donald E. *Vladimir Nabokov.* New York: Frederick Ungar, 1974. Sees *Lolita* as a serious love story. Dualities abound.

Moynahan, Julian. *Vladimir Nabokov.* Minneapolis: University of Minnesota Press, 1971. *Lolita* joins the tradition of novels about the quest for the American dream.

Nakhimosvsky, A., and S. Paperno, eds. *An English-Russian Dictionary of Nabokov's Lolita.* Ann Arbor, Mich.: Ardis, 1982. Language usage and stylistics.

Bibliography

Packman, David. *Vladimir Nabokov: The Structure of Literary Desire.* Columbia: University of Missouri Press, 1982. A poststructuralist reading. *Lolita* replays the detective genre. The reader and Humbert become sleuths in reflexive linguistic manipulation. Humbert's desire for Lolita *in* text doubles reader's desire for narrative resolution *of* text.

Page, Norman, ed. *Nabokov: The Critical Heritage.* London: Routledge & Kegan Paul, 1982. Reviews of Nabokov's work, 1934–77.

Parker, Stephen Jan, ed. *Nabokovian.* Lawrence: University of Kansas Press, 1984–, formerly (1978–84) *Vladimir Nabokov Research Newsletter.* Semiannual journal.

———. *Understanding Vladimir Nabokov.* Columbia: University of South Carolina Press, 1987. Introduction.

Proffer, Carl. *Keys to Lolita.* Bloomington: University of Indiana Press, 1968. Companion to Appel's annotations in *The Annotated Lolita.*

Rampton, David. *Vladimir Nabokov: A Critical Study of the Novels.* Cambridge: Cambridge University Press, 1984. Humanist reevaluation of *Lolita.*

Stegner, Page. *Escape into Aesthetics: The Art of Vladimir Nabokov.* New York: Dial, 1966. First and still first-class book on Nabokov. *Lolita* asks reader for compassionate understanding of Humbert's and Lolita's suffering.

Toker, Leona. *Nabokov: The Mystery of Literary Structures.* Ithaca: Cornell University Press, 1989. Examines the moral significance of the rhetoric of reader entrapment in *Lolita.* Humane emphasis on Lolita.

Articles

Amis, Martin. "*Lolita* Reconsidered." *Atlantic,* September 1992, 109–20. Reevaluation emphasizing death theme, Humbert's narcissism, humor, Lolita as America, prevalence of dolls and mannequins.

Bruss, Elizabeth W. "Vladimir Nabokov: Illusions of Reality and the Reality of Illusions." In *Autobiographical Acts: The Changing Situation of a Literary Genre,* 127–62. Baltimore: Johns Hopkins University Press, 1976. Humbert, continually switching genres, comes to understand the unreality of the autobiographical act.

Butler, Diana. "*Lolita* Lepidoptera." *New World Writing* 16 (1960): 58–84. Reprinted in *Critical Essays on Vladimir Nabokov,* edited by Phyllis A. Roth, 59–74. Boston: G. K. Hall & Co., 1984. Seminal study of butterflies in *Lolita.* Extended by Joann Karges in *Nabokov's Lepidoptera: Genres and Genera.* Ann Arbor, Mich.: Ardis, 1984.

Clifton, Gladys M. "Humbert Humbert and the Limits of Artistic License." In *Nabokov's Fifth Arc,* edited by J. E. Rivers and Charles Nicol, 153–70. Austin: University of Texas Press, 1982. Nabokov succeeds in writing comedy about serious subjects by making Lolita resilient and Humbert as long-suffering as much as any moralist might wish.

Dupee, F. W. "*Lolita* in America," *Encounter* (February 1959): 30–35. Publishing history.

Frosch, Thomas R. "Parody and Authenticity in *Lolita.*" In *Nabokov's Fifth Arc,* edited by J. E. Rivers and Charles Nicol, 171–87. Austin: University of Texas Press, 1982. *Lolita* participates in metaparody attempting to move beyond parody toward originality.

Karl, Frederick R. "Hawkes and Nabokov in the Fifties." In *American Fictions: 1940–1980,* 223–27. New York: Harper and Row, 1983. *Lolita* celebrates the counterfeit.

Pearce, Richard. "Nabokov's Black(Hole) Humor: *Lolita* and *Pale Fire.*" In *Comic Relief: Humor in Contemporary American Literature,* edited by Sarah Blacher Cohen, 28–44. Urbana: University of Illinois Press, 1978. Connects medieval rituals of revelry with Nabokov's "diabolical strategy" to deconstruct our ability to form judgments.

Robbe-Grillet, Alain. "Note sur la notion d'itinéraire dans *Lolita.*" *L'arc* 24 (1964): 37–38. Humbert's wandering is as much psychological as physical.

Shute, J. P. "Nabokov and Freud: The Play of Power." *Modern Fiction Studies* 30 (1984): 637–50. The textual battle for empowerment between these titans.

Tamir-Ghez, Nomi. "The Art of Persuasion in Nabokov's *Lolita.*" *Poetics Today* 1 (1979): 65–83. Reprinted in *Critical Essays on Vladimir Nabokov,* edited by Phyllis A. Roth, 157–76. Boston: G. K. Hall & Co., 1984. Extensive analysis of the rhetorical manipulations Humbert uses to sway the reader in his favor.

Tekiner, Christina. "Time in *Lolita.*" *Modern Fiction Studies* 25 (1979): 463–69. Argues that Humbert's last meeting with Lolita and Quilty's murder never really happened.

Trilling, Lionel. "The Last Lover." *Encounter* 11 (October 1958): 9–19. Reprinted in *Vladimir Nabokov's Lolita,* edited by Harold Bloom, 5–11. New York: Chelsea House, 1987. States *Lolita* is an ambiguous portrait of love, with antecedents in the courtly tradition.

Bibliographies

Juliar, Michael. *Vladimir Nabokov: A Descriptive Bibliography.* New York: Garland, 1986. Most complete bibliography of Nabokov's writings. Also list of books touching on Nabokov through 1985.

Parker, Stephen Jan, et al. "Nabokov Annual Bibliography." *Vladimir Nabokov Newsletter* and *Nabokovian.* Annual update.

Schuman, Samuel. *Vladimir Nabokov: A Reference Guide.* Boston: G. K. Hall, 1979. Annotated bibliography of Nabokov criticism from 1931 to 1977.

Index

139

Index

Index

The Author

Lance Olsen is director of the creative writing program and associate professor at the University of Idaho. He first read *Lolita* in 1977, the year Vladimir Nabokov died in Switzerland, while working toward his B.A. in English at the University of Wisconsin, and it was love at first sight. He went on to receive his M.F.A. from the Iowa Writers Workshop, and his M.A. and Ph.D. from the University of Virginia. He has taught at the University of Iowa, the University of Virginia, and the University of Kentucky. He is the author of the critical studies *Ellipse of Uncertainty: An Introduction to Postmodern Fantasy* (1987), *Circus of the Mind in Motion: Postmodernism and the Comic Vision* (1990), and *William Gibson* (1992); the novels *Live from Earth* (1991) and *Tonguing the Zeitgeist* (1994); the short-story collections *My Dates with Franz* (1993) and *Scherzi, I Believe* (1994); and, with Jeff Worley, the poetry chapbook *Natural Selections* (1993).